Krishna's Mercy

The Flag of Devotion

Daily articles from June/July 2009

All content authored by Sonal Pathak

Red Tape

It seems that if you want to get anything done in today's world, you're forced to encounter endless bureaucracy and red-tape. Take owning a car for example. After putting in hours of practice and passing a road test to obtain a driver's license, buying a car is another ordeal in and of itself. Aside from the actual purchase, there is insurance, registration, titles and taxes to pay for. Then once you own the car, you must re-register it at given intervals and have it inspected annually.

Whether it's buying a car, starting a business, hiring an employee, or even travelling to foreign countries, it seems that regulation is at an all time high. There is even bureaucracy involved with obtaining contact lenses now. The government restricts people from purchasing contact lenses who haven't had an eye exam in the past year, even if they currently wear contacts. The need for regulation and red-tape arises from the belief that everyone is a cheater. Not just the government, but most people in society have a natural inclination to be suspicious of others. We immediately assume everyone is a suspect and is trying to cheat us, so we enact laws that try to protect ourselves from them.

The Vedas, the ancient scriptures of India, give us a hint as to why we are like this. They tell us that human beings possess four primary defects. We have imperfect senses, we have a tendency to be illusioned, we have a propensity to commit mistakes, and we have a tendency to cheat. Since we cheat and commit mistakes ourselves, we naturally assume that others are the same way.

Another reason we are more suspicious nowadays is because of the rise of the mode of passion, known as tamo guna. In the Bhagavad-gita, Lord Krishna describes the tamo guna this way:

"The mode of passion is born of unlimited desires and longings, O son of Kunti, and, on account of this, one is bound to material, fruitive activities." (Bg, 14.7)

In this advanced technological age, there is ample opportunity for sense gratification. Once we satisfy one desire, another one invariably arises leaving us never truly satisfied. This constant craving for sense gratification leads us to lose our judgment. When we constantly crave something, we naturally don't want others to have it, and thus we become suspicious of others, thinking that they are honing in on our territory. Waiting in line at a restaurant or retail store, we become suspicious of other people, thinking that they will try to cut is in line. This all stems from the increased mode of passion. Lord Krishna also says:

"It is lust only, Arjuna, which is born of contact with the material modes of passion and later transformed into wrath; and which is the all-devouring, sinful enemy of this world. As fire is covered by smoke, as a mirror is covered by dust, or as the embryo is covered by the womb, similarly, the living entity is covered by different degrees of this lust." (Bg, 3.37-38)

The remedy for all this is very simple. We simply have to change our desires from the material to the spiritual. Our material senses can never be satisfied. It is not until we try to satisfy our spiritual senses that we will actually be happy. In this age, Lord Chaitanya instructed us that the best way of satisfying our spiritual senses to always chant:

"Hare Krishna Hare Krishna, Krishna Krishna, Hare Hare, Hare Rama Hare Rama, Rama Rama, Hare Hare"

When we chant the holy name of God, we forget our insatiable material desires and we gradually cleanse ourselves. Constantly placing the mind at the lotus feet of Lord Krishna, and reading about His wonderful pastimes, and picturing His beautiful face, we achieve liberation in this very life. As liberated souls, we view everyone equally, for we are all part and parcel of Lord Krishna. The tendency to cheat and be suspicious of others will be gone and we can all live peacefully.

Feeding the Hungry

In America today the hungry are fed through generous contributions made from citizens to various charitable institutions. The government also offers a food stamp program for the poor which is funded through taxes collected from the general population. While these programs may seem nice, they are not ideal.

The Vedas tell us that it is the responsibility of people in the grihashta ashrama to offer food in charity to others. A person's life is divided into four stages or ashramas, they being brahmacharya (celibate student life), grihastha (householder or family life), vanaprastha (retired family life) and sannyasa (the renounced order of life). Of all these stages, only those in the grihastha ashrama are supposed to give in charity, and people in the other three stages are the recipients of said donations.

According to the Mahabharata, the primary duties of a householder are to feed the gods and to feed guests. Householders engage in fruitive activity earning money, so it is recommended for them to use the fruits of their labor toward offering food to Krishna, or God. They are also required to host as many guests as possible. Shrila Prabhupada says that prior to eating, a householder is supposed to go out in the street and ask if anybody is hungry. The needy then come over and the householder serves them.

In today's age of Kali, we are all very suspect of each other. Married people often don't like to invite guests over because it is a burden to them. They think, "Well, so and so never invite us over to their house, so why should we call them over to ours?" This kind of tit-for-tat mentality is not prescribed by the scriptures. In Sanskrit, such people are referred to as *kripanahs*, or misers. The Ebenezer Scrooge character from the classic Charles Dickens short story "A Christmas Carol" is a famous example of a miser. Mr. Scrooge was a very unhappy and stingy businessman who paid his workers low wages and never gave money to charity. Through the miracle of Christmas and visits by three ghosts, he eventually changed his ways, but his last name is synonymous today with miserliness.

The Vedas advise everyone, especially the grihasthis, to avoid miserly behavior. A householder earns tremendous spiritual merit by hosting guests and feeding them sumptuously. A guest is to be received very warmly, offered a nice place to sit, and given sumptuous foodstuff to partake of. Householders are not supposed to eat until after the guest has finished eating. In this way, married couples purify themselves by eating the remnants of the offered food.

It is actually considered a great sin for a householder to receive a guest improperly. A famous example of this can be found in the Mahabharata. The five Pandava brothers, cousins to Lord Krishna, were serving an exile period in the forest when they were visited by Durvasa Muni, a great Brahmana who had brought a large group of fellow sages with Him. The Pandavas and their wife Drapaudi had just finished their midday meal, so there was no food available to serve their exalted guests. Fearing the wrath of the Brahmanas, Draupadi prayed to Krishna to alleviate the situation, and the Lord obliged. While the sages were bathing in a nearby river, Lord Krishna appeared at the scene and took a morsel of food that happened to still be in the serving bowl used by the Pandavas. The Lord then declared that His hunger was satisfied and miraculously the hunger of all the sages was satisfied at the same time. The sages returned from their bath and declared that they were pleased with the hospitality they received from Drapaudi, relieving her of any sin she might have incurred.

Though the ideal householder life may be difficult to implement in this age, the best thing a family can do is to become devotees of Lord Krishna and offer all their food to Him prior to eating. This prasadam should also be distributed to as many friends, family, and neighbors as possible. Through this system, there is no need for government programs or food donation charities. In this way, the householders can perform the highest service to their fellow man and satisfy society's real hunger, the hunger for spiritual life.

Curing the Fever

When we are struck with a raging fever, it seems that all hope is lost. Our body's temperature rapidly increases and it seems that there is pain everywhere. We feel chills throughout our body and it is difficult to even get up out of bed. That's where medicine comes in. A simple over-the-counter pain killer comes to our rescue. Shortly after taking a few pills, our body produces a burst of perspiration and our fever breaks. The fever is gone and we are no longer in discomfort.

In a similar manner, we living entities have been entwined in the raging fever known as material nature since time immemorial. We persevere through good times and bad, extreme heat and cold, happiness and distress, and victory and defeat, for these are the dualities of material nature. We are constantly looking for ways to alleviate our current pains and displeasures. At the same time, we make plans to hopefully avoid suffering these same ailments in the future. Hankering after the things we want, we lament when we don't get them. Whatever adjustments we make, material nature always manages to foil our plans and through our karma, we are forced to accept one body after another in a perpetual cycle of birth and death known as reincarnation.

The Vedas tell us that the only permanent cure to this fever is to become God conscious. One whose mind is fixed on serving the Supreme Lord no longer is bothered by the desires of the senses. In the Bhagavad-gita, Lord Krishna says:

"One who is thus transcendentally situated at once realizes the Supreme Brahman. He never laments nor desires to have anything; he is equally disposed to every living entity. In that state he attains pure devotional service unto Me." (Bg, 18.54)

To become transcendentally situated requires practice. The best and easiest way to practice transcendental realization is to repeatedly chant God's names in a loving way, in what is known as mantra meditation.

In our everyday affairs, if we want to stay focused on a task and not let our minds be diverted, we create a mantra that we constantly recite to remind ourselves of the task at hand. In a similar manner, successfully achieving spiritual realization also requires a mantra that must be repeated. Lucky for us, the Vedas supply us with thousands of them, with the most effective one being the Maha-mantra:

"Hare Krishna Hare Krishna, Krishna Krishna, Hare Hare, Hare Ram Hare Rama, Rama Rama, Hare Hare."

In this age, it is advisable to follow the prescriptions of the most respected spiritual doctor, Lord Shri Krishna Chaitanya Mahaprabhu, who advised everyone, irrespective of race, creed, gender, religion, or nationality, to constantly chant this Maha-mantra. Through chanting we come into direct contact with God, and we lose our material desires. The main symptom of a fever is the unnatural increase of the body's internal temperature. The symptom of the fever of material nature is our constant hankering and lamenting. Just as medicine returns our body to its normal temperature, the chanting of the holy names of God returns the spirit soul to the transcendental platform, which is its natural position.

Krishna is For Everyone

13

Question: "How can you (Krishna's Mercy) support a military that commits violence in order to protect a society which revolves around materialism?"

Answer:

God and His teachings are for everyone. One shouldn't make distinctions as to who is allowed to receive His message and who isn't. We living entities are all His children and are all equally entitled to have an opportunity to serve Him.

Judging the actions of military servicemen on the material platform is a mistake. The concept of good and bad actually doesn't exist in the spiritual realm. In actuality, any and all fruitive activity is on the same level since it has karma associated with it. Karma refers to any activity performed which has a material consequence attached to it, be it good or bad. Whether one is engaged in pious or impious works, as long as they are acting on the material plane, there really is no good or bad.

Now this doesn't mean that we should all behave impiously. Material nature is composed of three *gunas* or qualities, known as goodness, passion, and ignorance. All karmic activity can be classified into one of these three categories. However, above these three modes is pure goodness, which is completely spiritual in nature. Pure goodness, known as *suddha sattva*, is characterized by any activity done for the satisfaction of the Supreme Lord, Shri Krishna. Bhakti yoga, or devotional service, is the only good activity since it involves service to God, thus making it completely immune to the reactions of karma. This is the aim of human life, to become devotees of Krishna. One who is devoted to God and thinks of Him at the time of death, is completely absolved of all their sins and thus never returns to this material world. Krishna is by nature impartial to all living entities.

He makes an exception however, for His devotees as stated in the Bhagavad-gita:

"I envy no one, nor am I partial to anyone. I am equal to all. But whoever renders service unto Me in devotion is a friend, is in Me, and I am also a friend to him." (Bg. 9.29)

The *brahmanas* are considered the highest class in society because they have dedicated their lives to serving God. It is the duty of the *brahmanas* and all devotees of Krishna to spread the message of the Lord to everyone regardless of cast, color, or creed. One's standing in society or one's occupation should be of no concern, since it is one's character which determines whether or not they are fit to serve Krishna. We need only look to Vedic literature to see examples of this principle in practice.

The Bhagavad-gita, the most famous spiritual scripture in the Vedic tradition, was spoken by Lord Krishna, God Himself, to His cousin and dear friend Arjuna on the battlefield of Kurukshetra. Arjuna was a *kshatriya* by trade, meaning he was a military man whose duty it was to administer justice. The Bharata War involved a dispute between two sets of cousin brothers, the Pandavas and Kauravas, over who had the right to rule over a kingdom. Arjuna, the leading warrior on the side of the Pandava brothers, was feeling weak hearted just prior to the war's commencement, not wanting to commit violence against family members in order to win the material comforts of a kingdom. It was Krishna who convinced him otherwise, informing him that it was the duty of a kshatriya to fight and defend his territory. Krishna did not think to Himself, "Oh this man is devolved in violence simply for sense gratification, thus I must not instruct Him on the proper rules of conduct." On the contrary, the Lord judged Arjuna based on his qualities. Arjuna was a great devotee of God and very pure hearted, and it was for this reason that the Lord viewed him as a worthy recipient of the teachings of the Bhagavad-gita.

As the war proceeded, Arjuna would end up mortally wounding the opposing army's greatest warrior, Bhishma. Bhishma was the grandfather of both the Pandavas and Kauravas, and thus was respected by everyone. While lying on the battlefield about to die, he fixed his mind on Lord Krishna. The Lord, being all-sensing, knew this was happening, so He instructed Yudhishthira, Arjuna's older brother, to go to Bhishma and take instruction from him on spiritual matters. On the surface, this appears very surprising. Lord Krishna served as Arjuna's charioteer, thus He somewhat played a role in Bhishma's defeat. As previously mentioned, the concept of good guys and bad guys didn't apply in this situation, since Bhishma was a great devotee, who was performing His duty by fighting nobly for his side. His pure devotion to Krishna and firm grasp of Vedic teachings endeared him to the Lord. It was for this reason that though defeated in battle, Bhishma gained everlasting fame by instructing Yudhisthira on dharma and devotion to Krishna just prior to quitting his body.

Another famous example of the Lord's mercy can be found in the Ramayana. Krishna appeared on earth as Lord Rama many thousands of years ago for the purpose of killing the evil *rakshasa* demon Ravana. Ravana had propitiated various demigods and was using the boons received from them to wreak havoc throughout the world and disrupt the sacrifices of the great sages. As part of his dastardly deeds, he even kidnapped Lord Rama's wife, Sita, while the couple were serving an exile period in the forest. This gave Lord Rama the excuse he needed to march to Ravana's kingdom and take him on in battle. Just prior to embarking for Lanka, the island where Ravana had set up his kingdom, Lord Rama's army was visited by Vibhishana, Ravana's younger brother. By birth both Ravana and Vibhishana were *rakshasas*, a race of demons evil by nature, who feast on the flesh of others, and who involve themselves in the art of black magic. Vibhishana, however, was a devotee of Lord Rama and he tried his hardest to persuade Ravana to return Sita to the Lord. After Ravana refused to listen to him, Vibhishana decided he would surrender himself unto Lord Rama and ask to join His side. When Vibhishana arrived at their camp, all the members of Rama's army were very suspicious. They were hesitant to accept Vibhishana due to his being a *rakshasa*, but Lord Rama overlooked that fact. Since Rama knew him to be a great devotee, the Lord accepted him wholeheartedly, welcoming him to their side. After Lord Rama defeated and killed Ravana, He installed Vibhishana as the new king of Lanka. Thus his devotion to the Lord paid off.

When Krishna appeared on earth as Lord Chaitanya some five hundred years ago in India, His immediate expansion, Baladeva, also appeared with Him in the form of Nityananda Prabhu. Lord Chaitanya inaugurated the sankirtana movement in India, travelling throughout the country chanting the holy names of God to everyone He would meet. Nityananda Prabhu was part of His group, and one day while preaching in the street, He was attacked by two drunkard brothers named Jagai and Madhai. Madhai wanted no part in hearing about the glories of Lord Krishna, so he threw a pot at Nityananda's head, causing Him to start bleeding. Lord Chaitanya became very angry upon hearing of this incident and wanted to take out His wrath on the two brothers, but it was Nityananda Prabhu who immediately stepped in and forgave them. Taken aback by Nityananda's kindness and mercy, the two brothers immediately changed their ways and became disciples of Lord Chaitanya.

As we can see, God is very merciful. His name, fame, and glories should be distributed to everyone. Most in society today are involved primarily in acts of sense gratification, thinking only of the demands of the body. In the United States, the military is an all-volunteer group of men and women. Deployed servicemen put their lives on the line every day in order to protect the livelihoods of their fellow citizens. Through such service, they transcend the natural attachment that people have to their own bodies and their way of life. This selflessness is a very good quality to have, since understanding that we are not this body is the first step in spiritual realization. In the Vedic tradition, the Sanskrit term *aham brahmasmi,* meaning "I am Brahman" or "I am a spirit soul who is part and parcel of God.", is the first lesson taught to aspiring transcendentalists. Our bodies are temporary, but our souls are not. The soul is eternal and never dies.

"This individual soul is unbreakable and insoluble, and can be neither burned nor dried. He is everlasting, all-pervading, unchangeable, immovable and eternally the same. It is said that the soul is invisible, inconceivable, immutable, and unchangeable. Knowing this, you should not grieve for the body." (Lord Krishna speaking to Arjuna, Bhagavad-gita 2.24-25)

Since the brave men and women serving in the military have already risen above bodily designations, they are ideal candidates for receiving spiritual instruction. In the classic system of *varnashrama dharma* (the four divisions of society and time periods in one's life recommended by the Vedas), the *kshatriyas* were in charge of the government and the *brahmanas* served as their chief advisors. This system desperately needs to be reintroduced in society, since brave warriors versed in the science of bhakti yoga would make ideal government leaders. If the government is filled with God conscious people, then the rest of society will soon follow. Hopefully through Krishna's mercy, this ideal system can one day become a reality.

Expert Counseling

In today's day and age, it is very common for people to seek counseling and therapy from psychologists and other trained professionals. The idea behind such a practice is that a counselor can act as a neutral party and thus provide guidance and reassurance during troubled times. Since counselors are not people that we know very well, we feel more open towards the idea of sharing our problems with them.

In general, seeking this sort of help is a last resort for people who don't have any close friends that they can turn to. The Vedas tells us that Lord Krishna, God, is our Supreme Friend and is always there to help us. God can be realized in three distinct features. In His first feature, Krishna acts as the impersonal Brahman, which is a sort of energy that pervades all of creation. The impersonalist philosophers and yogis worship this feature of God, for they wish to merge into Brahman. In the second feature, the Lord expands Himself as the Paramatma, or Supersoul, residing in the hearts of all living entities.

Every living entity has two souls within them: the individual soul which represents one's identity, and the Supersoul which is God's expansion. The Paramatma acts as a witness to all our activities and getting in touch with this feature enables us to finally realize God's third feature as Bhagavan, or the Supreme Personality of Godhead. We all have consciousness that pervades our body, for that is the very essence of being alive. The Paramatma is the Supreme Consciousness. If we dovetail our consciousness with the Supreme Consciousness, then all our problems will be solved. We will no longer require any help from uninterested counselors or therapists. So this begs the question, "How do we get in touch with the Supersoul?"

For the benefit of the devotees, Krishna expands Himself into innumerable forms such as His various avatars, deities, and Paramatma. Even a picture of the Lord is a representation of one of His forms. In this current age, the Lord is so merciful that he incarnates in the form of His holy name. So just by saying the word Krishna, or even reading it, we come into direct contact with Him. There is no difference between God and His names. The Shrimad-Bhagavatam contains the famous story of Ajamila, a devotee who went astray but was saved from going to hell due to uttering the name Narayana at the time of his death. Narayana is one of Krishna's names, and Ajamila had the good fortune of naming his son after Him. Ajamila was a great devotee in his early life, but he fell down from his exalted position due to association with a prostitute. In his old age, as his life breath was leaving him, Ajamila called out for his son, and since it was the also the name of God, he was saved from going to hell by Lord Vishnu's agents, the Vishnuduttas. Instead of suffering for his sinful actions, Ajamila eventually ascended to Krishna's spiritual planet.

By reciting God's names in a loving manner, we gradually come closer to His Paramatma feature that resides inside us. If we are sincere in our chanting, God's Paramatma feature will lead us to one of His authorized representatives, a spiritual master, who will guide us in such a way that all our problems will be eliminated. The spiritual master is the most expert counselor. He is a pure devotee of Krishna, making him kind, compassionate, and intelligent enough to give us the proper prescription for our ailments. Unlike counseling which can go on for years and years without ever coming close to solving anything, the spiritual master's instructions from the very beginning aim to tackle the root of our problems, which is our forgotten relationship with God. As soon as we take the necessary steps to reconnect with Him, the healing process will commence.

Cow Protection

American life is all about freedom. The Pilgrims settled on this land hundreds of years ago to enjoy freedom and to escape an oppressive government in Europe. Living in America means we can do what we want, whenever we want to without worrying about others interfering with us. As long as we don't infringe on the rights of others, we are free to act as we wish.

One way Americans and others around the world enjoy freedom is by eating meat, especially beef. Cows and other animals are raised on farms with the express purpose of being sent to slaughterhouses. Eating beef, steak in particular, is a classic American tradition, with the quintessential family meal consisting of "meat and potatoes". The beef industry even runs television advertisements where the tag line is "Beef. It's what's for dinner." There are various grades of beef, based on the type of cow, how it is raised, and how it is fed. Simply eating meat is not enough, for people are more than willing to shell out extra money to feast themselves on high quality beef such as Kobe and Wagyu.

In principle, having the independence to act as we wish is not a bad thing. It is the natural yearning of the human spirit to be free. However, with freedom comes responsibility. If we maintain our bodies through unnecessary violence, then the laws of karma dictate that we will be forced to suffer in the future. God has given us an abundance of food grains for our sustenance. Cows play their part as well by freely providing us milk. In the Vedic tradition, cows are to be respected. Many people mistakenly believe that Hindus worship cows as gods, but that is not the case. Cows are respected and treated on the same level as one's own mother since they provide us milk. Our mothers nourish us as infants with milk from their breasts, and in the same way one's body can be nourished simply from the milk of a cow. According to the Vedas, there are seven mothers: the birth mother, the guru's wife, the wife of a brahmana (priest), the wife of a king, a nurse, the earth, and a cow. Now we wouldn't ever think of killing our own mother, so why should we kill cows?

Cows are killed so that people can satisfy the desires of the tongue. As the famous proverb says "As you sow so shall you reap", one committing unnecessary violence simply to satisfy the taste buds will naturally by forced to suffer the same fate in the future. This is only fair. The need to respect and protect cows shouldn't be a difficult concept for us to grasp. Many of us keep pets in the home, such as cats and dogs. We view them as the essence of innocence, since they kindly serve as our companions and ask little in return. "Dog is man's best friend" so the saying goes. People love their pets so much that they often treat them better than they do their friends and family. It is not uncommon for pet owners to take many pictures of their cat or dog and show them off to their friends, as if the pets were their own children. Owners will go to great lengths to keep their pets happy, gladly inconveniencing themselves by regularly taking the dogs for walks or by feeding gourmet meals to their cats. Cows should be given the same level of respect.

Just because the meat of a cow tastes good, doesn't mean that they are any less innocent than a cat or a dog. Unlike a cat or a dog, cows actually provide us things of tangible value. Cows don't bother anyone and the milk they freely provide can be used to prepare hundreds of varieties of palatable foodstuffs. In the Vedic system, a person's wealth is determined by how many cows they have. One simply requires a small plot of land and a few cows and their economic problems are solved. This is a much more secure lifestyle than possessing large quantities of paper currency, which can devalue at any time. The recent worldwide economic crisis proves this fact. In the Vedic system, the *brahmanas*, or priestly class of men, are to live very meagerly, focusing all their time on serving God. Knowing this, *kshatriya* kings would regularly give away kine to the brahmanas so that they wouldn't have to worry about food.

Any occasion, good or bad, would always be marked by the giving away of cows to *brahmanas*, as that is considered the highest form of charity.

Cows are also considered valuable because they provide butter which is used in Vedic sacrifices. The material world is governed by the demigods, who serve as Lord Krishna's chief ministers. By propitiating them, man is provided with rain which serves as the catalyst for food production. The demigods are worshiped in elaborate fire sacrifices called *yajnas*, where clarified butter, or ghee, is poured on the fire as an oblation. These sacrifices would not be possible were it not for the ghee. In this way, cows can be considered the sustainers of life.

Once we stop respecting our mothers, we eventually lose respect for other forms of life. This is evidenced by the increase in the practice of abortion. In order to satisfy the demands of the tongue, innocent cows are sent to slaughterhouses. So it shouldn't surprise anyone that people would resort to killing innocent children in the womb in order to satisfy the desires of the genitals. Cows are very dear to Lord Krishna, who is also known as Govinda, which means "one who gives pleasure to the cows". When the Lord personally came to earth around five thousand years ago, he grew up in a cowherd family, and he would regularly take the family cows out to the pasturing grounds as a child. One will often see the Lord depicted in pictures standing next to cows. Thus by respecting cows, we are following God's example. There is no higher form of religion than to follow the instructions and traditions set forth by Lord Krishna.

A Happy Home

"**The best process for making the home pleasant is Krishna consciousness. If one is in full Krishna consciousness, he can make his home very happy because this process of Krishna consciousness is very easy. One need only chant Hare Krishna, Hare Krishna, Krishna Krishna, Hare Hare/Hare Rama, Hare Rama, Rama Rama, Hare Hare, accept the remnants of foodstuffs offered to Krishna, have some discussion on books like Bhagavad-gita and Shrimad-Bhagavatam, and engage oneself in Deity worship. These four will make one happy. One should train the members of his family in this way. The family members can sit down morning and evening and chant together**" (Shrila Prabhupada, Bg 13.8-12 Purport)

In today's society, especially in Western countries, divorce is a very common practice resorted to by couples having problems in their marriage. Due to the high divorce rate, many churches will not allow people to get married in their church unless they undergo a series of counseling sessions. This course, known as "Pre-Cana", is given as a way of helping ensure the solvency of the marriage. Couples are taught about the institution of marriage, what to expect, and how to get along with each other. The concepts of shared love, responsibility, and conflict resolution are discussed along with other topics. Many local governments also provide similar instructions to couples when they apply for marriage licenses. Many people even go so far as to sign prenuptial agreements, hoping that this will prevent their spouse from potentially coming after their assets through the divorce system.

While these attempts are very nice and well intentioned, we see that many couples still end up divorcing even after going through such extraordinary preventative measures. In actuality, the concept of divorce is a modern man made creation. According to the Vedas, a marriage is a bond between a man and a woman that exists for life. Even if the husband takes to the renounced order of life, *sannyasa*, he is still considered married to his wife.

In the Vedic tradition, boys are married as soon as they have any inkling for sex life. The same holds true for girls. In this way, sex life is allowed, but only in a regulated manner inside of a marriage. There is no concept of boyfriend/girlfriend or the free association between men and women. Marriage occurs through the arrangement of the parents. A girl's parents will compare the qualities of their daughter with that of the potential son-in-law. Both families compare each other's lineage to make sure that the family traditions and values match up. Married life is known as the *grihastha* ashrama. In the Vedic system of varnashrama dharma, a person's life is to be divided into four successive stages, each of which is conducive to achieving God realization. *Grihastha* is the second stage of life where ones lives as a householder with one's spouse and children. It immediately follows the stage of celibate student life, known as *brahmacharya*. Household life requires the wife to serve all the needs of the husband, and for the husband to provide full protection for his wife. This allows for a peaceful life where both parties can make spiritual advancement simultaneously.

Disagreements naturally occur, but no thought is given to divorce. Both parties understand from the beginning what their role is. In the modern system of love marriages, the wife is always asking herself if the husband still loves her. The husband is always asking himself if his wife is devoted to her. Much effort is taken to maintain the "romantic spark". For couples in the Vedic system, these questions don't arise since there is a sense of duty that exists from the very beginning. Both the husband and wife are working towards a cause higher than themselves.

Whether it is a love marriage or a Vedic style marriage, the best way to ensure a successful household life is for both husband and wife to constantly chant the holy names of God together. Married couples should rise early, perform deity worship, chant together, and then eat prasadam. The same process can be repeated in the evening. Even the children can get involved. Young children are the essence of innocence, as they haven't developed many of the inhibitions that adults have. Thus, they will take very nicely to serving the Lord by accompanying the parents in their chanting and offering of prayers and prasadam. Such activities will prove more valuable to children than watching television or playing video games.

According to the Shrimad-Bhagavatam, one should not be a king, a teacher, or a parent unless they can deliver their dependents from the repeated cycle of birth and death. People may have children for other reasons, many of which are very noble, but the highest service a parent can perform for a child is to make them Krishna, or God conscious. This will ensure that their child's birth will be their last one. Even the parents are benefitted from such a situation, since a truly devoted person can deliver many previous generations of family members. The great sage Bhagiratha brought Mother Ganga, the Ganges River, down from heaven to earth, thus delivering five previous generations of family members, including the sixty thousand sons of King Sagara.

If we water the roots of a tree, then automatically the branches and leaves are also fed. In the same way, if we provide nice service to Lord Krishna, the Supreme Personality of Godhead, then the needs of our friends and family are satisfied at the same time. If a husband and wife work together for the highest cause, then they will always be happy and secure in their marriage.

Renunciation Made Easy

"We don't simply prohibit that 'You don't do this,' but we supply something which is engaged by the senses and the mind, the intelligence, so that you do not require to be engaged otherwise." (Shrila Prabhupada, Lecture 690101BG.LA)

Religion is sometimes misunderstood as being something very restrictive, full of rigid rules and regulations that must strictly be adhered to. While there are many rules that exist, they serve only a beginning step, a way to guide a person to a much higher end goal.

Understanding God and learning to love Him is the real purpose and meaning behind religion. In the Vedas, this is referred to as *sanatana dharma*. *Sanatana* means that which has no beginning and no end, and *dharma* means duty or prescribed occupation. So the idea of religion really refers to the eternal occupation of man and not simply to blind faith.

Due to rapid advancements in technology, today's society has more free time to indulge in leisurely activities and sybaritic pursuits than generations past. We spend our free time watching movies, playing different sports, or surfing the internet. Many people focus all their free time on activities of intoxication, gambling, and chasing after sex life. If one becomes overly attached to these activities, they trap themselves in an endless cycle of mundane sense gratification that always leaves them wanting more.

These activities may be bad for us, but what else are we supposed to do with our free time? This is where bhakti yoga, or devotional service, comes in. Not to be confused with the modern day definition of yoga involving various breathing exercises and sitting postures, bhakti yoga is a way of life where all of one's activities are dovetailed with service to the Supreme. Instead of retreating to a mountain top and chanting the syllable *Om* over and over again, devotional service is a call to action.

In the Vedas, if one is serious about making spiritual progress, it is recommended that they abstain from the four pillars of sinful life: meat eating, illicit sex, intoxication, and gambling. Abruptly renouncing something, quitting it "cold turkey", isn't very easy for most of us to do. We have built up an attachment to sinful activity over many many births and it is very difficult to break free of them. To help us in our renunciation, the Vedas recommend that we constantly engage ourselves in God's service. By taking this approach, we will be so busy that we won't have any time for sinful activity. If we prepare all our food to be offered to Lord Krishna first, we will automatically stop eating meat, for the Lord does not accept food consisting of animal flesh.

"If one offers Me with love and devotion a leaf, a flower, fruit or water, I will accept it." (Lord Krishna, Bhagavad-gita, 9.26)

If we engage ourselves in chanting His names and reading books about Him, we'll experience a feeling of bliss that surpasses any highs that we get from intoxication. By using our hard earned money to purchase nice flowers for the Lord's deity, or to construct nice temples for Him, or to support His devotees, we'll lose any desire we may have to gamble. The husband and wife serving the Lord together, performing various sacrifices and rituals in their home, will become even more committed to each other, losing any desire they may have for illicit sex life.

Renunciation is commonly viewed as an end-goal, something that we have to strive for. In actually, renunciation is automatically acquired by those actively engaged in a higher cause. If we gradually devote ourselves to God's service, our love for Him will increase, and our desire for sinful activity will diminish without us ever having to think about renouncing anything.

Right By Your Side

"Regarded by her husband, Sita of dark eyes, and intent upon her husband's welfare, followed Him to the entrance and said, 'I shall be ministering to you, seeing you initiated, engaged in ceremonies, wearing excellent deer skin for cloth and carrying horns in my hands.'" (Sita Devi speaking to Lord Rama, Valmiki Ramayana, Ayodhya Kand, Sec 21)

Lord Rama, the incarnation of God in the Treta Yuga, was all set to be installed as the new king of Ayodhya by His father, Maharaja Dashratha. On the day set for the Lord's installation, a messenger came to the palace where He and His wife lived and informed Him that the king wanted to see Him. Unaware that the plans had changed and that Bharata, Rama's younger brother, was instead going to be installed as the new king, the Lord set off for His father's palace. Just prior to leaving, He informed His wife, Sita Devi, that He would be right back and to not worry. In response, Sita Devi addressed her husband as noted above.

Sita's statement to her husband represents the one thing every person wants from their spouse, support. As long as the wife is supportive, the husband is happy and vice versa. Sadly, the level of support shown by Sita is not always present in marriages. Many times, it is seen that a husband or wife can become jealous when their spouse suddenly comes upon good fortune. This is quite natural as we all have a little bit of envy inside of us. According to the Vedas, mankind suffers from four distinct defects, those being the propensity to cheat, the tendency to be easily illusioned, possessing imperfect senses, and being prone to committing mistakes. Greed, wrath, envy, and hypocrisy also naturally exist in everyone in varying degrees.

In any close relationship such as a marriage, when one person's fortunes suddenly take a turn for the better, the other person often feels slighted and left out. We all want to be important and make a difference. Each of us is special and knowing this, we want to matter in life. When we are involved in a close relationship with a loved one, we want to think of ourselves as the only source of pleasure for our significant other. Being in love or loving someone means surrendering everything unto them, be they a husband, wife, or significant other. Thus the lover voluntarily puts themselves in a subordinate position, requiring the reciprocation of love in order to feel happiness. Put into this dependent position, we hope that our loved one feels the same way that we do and is as equally dependent on us for their happiness. If our spouse or significant other suddenly becomes rich or famous, it is natural for us to worry that maybe they will derive more happiness from their newfound fame than they will from their relationship with us.

With Sita Devi, none of these feelings existed. Her husband was on the precipice of something really great. Lord Rama was born into one of the most famous dynasties in history, the Ikshvakus. They were all very pious rulers, and to take birth in that line was considered a great boon. Rama was the eldest and most cherished son of King Dashratha, so ascension to the throne was inevitable and eagerly anticipated by the citizens of Ayodhya. On the day set for her husband's installation, Sita reassured Him that she would be there right by His side, supporting Him throughout the ceremony. She wanted to let Him know that she would always be there for Him and that they would share this momentous occasion together.

According to the Vedic system, once married, a husband and wife equally share the same fate in this life and the next. They are considered to be one person. Even God, in His various forms, is always worshiped alongside His pleasure potency, who acts as His wife or eternal consort. Lord Krishna is worshiped with Shrimati Radharani, Lord Rama is worshipped with Sita Devi, Narayana (Vishnu) is worshiped with Lakshmi, and so on. Since they both share the same fate, it is in the best interest of the wife to make sure that the husband is always happy and performing his religious duties. For the husband, it is imperative that the wife always remain protected and feel safe, so that they can together perform their prescribed duties as householders. Those in the *grihastha* ashrama, householder life, are required to perform many Vedic sacrficies, or *yajnas,* as part of their samskaras (sacraments or religious training). Since they are in the only stage of life where fruitive activity is sanctioned, they are required to perform sacrifices and to be charitable to the rest of society. Sita Devi was well acquainted with this system, so she was ready for all the specific aspects of the installation ceremony. Since she was God's wife, she was pious right from her very birth and all her actions in life were exemplary.

Aside from acting as an ideal wife, Sita showed us the example of how to serve all of God's needs. The Vedas refer to the Supreme as *atmarama,* meaning one who is self-satisfied. He is in need of nothing, but through His mercy, He voluntarily places Himself in situations where His devotees can serve Him. This was the case with Sita Devi. He wanted everyone to see just how great a devotee she was. In order to glorify her and give her everlasting fame, He created situations where her dedication could be put on display.

When we see Lord Krishna's forms, especially that of Lord Vishnu, He always appears very opulent and beautifully dressed. His body is adorned with the Kaustubha gem, earrings, a flower garland, and other such paraphernalia. He is God after all so naturally He will be very beautiful, but actually the Lord appears this way due to the desire of His devotees. Just as car owners take very good care of their cars, washing them regularly and making them look very nice, the Lord's devotees love Him so much that they put His happiness and pleasure above their own. They want Him to have all the fame and glory and for Him to always be adorned with beautiful paraphernalia. In the spiritual world, Sita Devi is known as Lakshmi, the goddess of fortune. Sometimes the Lord is addressed as Madhava or Shripati, meaning the husband of the goddess of fortune. She is always by Lord Vishnu's side, massaging His feet and attending to His every need. Appearing on earth in the form of Sita, she assumed the same role. We would all be well served to follow her wonderful example and pledge our support to the Lord and His devotees. Though God is not always physically present before us, He deputes His pure devotees to serve as His bona fide representatives. By always keeping our minds on the lotus feet of the Supreme Lord and by offering our services to the great devotees like Hanumanji, Tulsidas, Shrila Prabhupada and others, we perform the highest service for the Lord.

Krishna's Mrdanga

Lord Chaitanya started the original sankirtana movement in India some five hundred years ago. Sankirtana is the process of congregationally chanting the holy names of the Lord and it is the process most recommended for people in this age. In Kali Yuga, people generally don't want to hear about God. If they meet a religious person they may think, "Whoah this person is crazy. They're one of those God freaks that's going to tell me what's wrong with my life and that I'm going to hell." This may in fact be the behavior of many preachers, but in the Vedic system this is not so. Brahmanas, the priestly class of society, are required to teach others on dharma and devotion to Lord Krishna in a compassionate manner, with equal regard for all living entities.

Now in the past, the brahmanas were automatically afforded the highest respect by the rest of society. Kings would maintain at least a few brahmanas in the royal court and they would take direction from them. The famous king of Ayodhya, Maharaja Dashratha, had the venerable sage Vashishta as his royal priest. Aside from listening to him, the king also gave respect to other brahmanas. One time, the sage Vishvamitra visited his kingdom and requested to have two of the king's sons, Rama and Lakshmana, accompany him for a short period in the forest. Lord Rama was an incarnation of Krishna and also the eldest son of Dashratha. He was very attached to Rama and felt that he wouldn't be able to handle separation from Him. He tried to get Vishvamitra to change his mind, but the sage insisted on having Rama since he required protection from the rakshasas that were ranging the forest. In the end, Dashratha acquiesced, for he was very pious and knew that the requests of the great sages should never be denied. Similarly, Vedic literature is full of many historical incidences relating to the venerable Narada Muni where people reformed their lives by following his instructions.

In today's age, the situation is reversed, where the truly saintly people are generally ignored. For this reason, Lord Chaitanya popularized the sankirtana movement, whereby God's name would be sung loudly throughout society. If people didn't want to hear discussions on the Bhagavad-gita or Ramayana, then they could still make spiritual progress by hearing the Lord's names melodiously sung. A key component of a sankirtana party is a mrdanga, which Wikipedia defines as "an Indian percussion instrument meaning 'beat and go'". The mrdanga player provides the beat, and along with a few kartal (cymbals) players and a lead singer, you have a sankirtana party. This movement has been very popular in India since its introduction by Lord Chaitanya, and now has become popular worldwide through the mercy of His Divine Grace A.C. Bhaktivedanta Swami Prabhupada.

Shrila Bhaktisiddhanta Saraswati Prabhupada often referred to the printing press as the *brhad-mrdanga,* or big mrdanga. He was a very big fan of it since it could quickly produce large quantities of Krishna conscious reading material that could be disseminated to the general public. He was the spiritual master of Shrila Prabhupada and he wanted very much for all his disciples to preach the cult of Lord Chaitanya Mahaprabhu throughout the world, especially in the Western countries. This was his direct request to Shril Prabhupada, and the swami took it to heart.

In the modern age, blogging has become a very popular means of promoting ideas and thoughts. In previous times, a person required the help of a newspaper or magazine in order to spread information about something. Without the help of mass distribution, people's exposure to opinions and commentary remained limited to what was seen on television and in local newspapers. The internet has brought about a change in the way information is gathered and disseminated. The weblog, or blog, has become an invaluable tool in allowing people to promote their ideas and businesses. A newspaper can host a blog to bring stories to readers even before the next issue of their paper hits newsstands. Most blogs allow for comments from readers and responses from other bloggers. This provides a much more in depth presentation of issues.

Though blogs already exists for just about every issue, the best use of a blog is to promote and educate others about God. In India, information about God, contained in the Vedas, was passed down from generation to generation through aural reception. The Vedas are also referred to as *shrutis*, meaning "that which is heard." With the new internet age, these same Vedic teachings can be distributed to the masses in written form in a very short amount of time. God has been very kind to allow us to take birth in an age where the internet is prominent. We should make the best use of such an opportunity by using the internet to spread His glories. This would have been the wish of Shrila Bhaktisiddhanta, so let's make him proud by using the internet as Krishna's mrdanga!

The Price is Right

42

"Whatever was possible to perform in the Satya Yuga by meditation and the Treta Yuga by offering of costly sacrifices, and in the Dvapara Yuga by offering prayers or archana in the temple, that can be made possible easily by *hari-kirtana*, by chanting the holy name of God." (Shrila Prabhupada, Lecture, 1966.05.25 NY)

Due to the recent downturn in the economy, many retail stores are going out of business. It is very common to see liquidation and going out of business sales around various shopping areas. Though not good for the retailers, these liquidation sales present a tremendous opportunity for bargain shoppers. Retail items are drastically discounted in price and shoppers often race to the stores to take advantage. Checkout lines are typically very long at these stores, with shoppers trying to grab as much cheap merchandise as they can.

In a similar fashion, the price of self-realization has been drastically reduced in this age of Kali. According to Vedic philosophy, each creation of the earth is divided into four time periods. During the first time period, known as the Satya Yuga, the level of dharma is at one hundred percent in society. People are completely pious, thus it is known as the Golden Age. With each successive age, dharma is reduced by one quarter its original strength. In the Kali Yuga, the age we are currently in, dharma is only at twenty five percent. For this reason, God has made the path to self-realization easier.

In previous ages, serving God required rigorous meditation, strict deity worship, or the performance of elaborate sacrifices. The practice of meditation is still very popular in the modern age, but this is not anything like the meditation practiced in the Satya Yuga. For one to practice meditation properly, one must strictly adhere to the rules enjoined in the *shashtras*, or scriptures. The first requirement is that one must be completely celibate. Meditation means concentration on the Supreme Lord, and having control over one's sexual desires is necessary in order for one to fully concentrate. Another requirement is that one must practice their meditation in a secluded place. This was told to Arjuna by Lord Krishna Himself.

"A transcendentalist should always try to concentrate his mind on the Supreme Self; he should live alone in a secluded place and should always carefully control his mind. He should be free from desires and feelings of possessiveness. To practice yoga, one should go to a secluded place and should lay kusha grass on the ground and then cover it with a deerskin and a soft cloth. The seat should neither be too high nor too low and should be situated in a sacred place. The yogi should then sit on it very firmly and should practice yoga by controlling the mind and the senses, purifying the heart and fixing the mind on one point." (Bhagavad-gita, 6.10-11)

As we can see, it is almost impossible for most people to follow these regulations today. In a similar manner, the elaborate sacrifices that were performed in the past are not so easy to put together today. The kings were very pious in previous times, so they would regular perform grand sacrifices such as the *ashvamedha* and *rajasuya*. Maharaja Dashratha, the king of Ayodhya, performed the *ashvamedha* sacrifice in order to obtain a son and he was thereby blessed by having Lord Rama, God Himself, take birth as his eldest son. The process recommended for the Dvapara Yuga was *archanam*, or deity worship. While this practice still exists today, it is not as widespread as it was in the Dvapara Yuga. Temple worship involves installing an *archa-vigraha*, or deity, of the Lord and then worshiping it in regular intervals throughout the day. A pujari, or priest, is in charge of maintaining and tending to the deity, and visitors to the temple come to see the Lord and offer their prayers to Him. Prasadam is also distributed. This process is still going on today but it really flourished during the Dvapara Yuga.

A.C. Bhaktivedanta Swami Prabhupada described the differences of the particular Yugas in this way:

"...in the Satya Yuga people used to realize self or used to elevate themselves to the highest perfection of life by meditation. You have heard the name of Valmiki Muni. Valmiki Muni, he meditated for sixty thousands of years. His whole body was covered by worms. ...gradually our life is being reduced...In the Satya Yuga, it is stated, that people used to live for one hundred thousands of years...And in the Treta-Yuga, ten thousand years. In the Dvapara Yuga one thousand years. And now it has come down to one hundred years in this Kali Yuga. That also, one hundred years is not completed. Now we are dying within sixty or seventy and gradually it will be reduced to twenty to thirty years. That is also mentioned. So what was possible in the Satya Yuga by meditation, that is not possible in this age. That is not possible. Therefore the methods have been made easier." (Lecture, 1966.05.25 NY)

In this age, Lord Chaitanya, who is Krishna Himself, introduced the process of sankirtana as the means for salvation. Sankirtana is the congregational chanting of the holy name of God. Lord Chaitanya instructed us to chant the maha-mantra, **"Hare Krishna Hare Krishna, Krishna Krishna, Hare Hare, Hare Rama Hare Rama, Rama Rama, Hare Hare"** as much as possible.

Unlike the methods of previous ages, sankirtana doesn't have any strict rules associated with it. One can chant at any time and at any place. One doesn't have to be in the renounced order of life or even be an adult. Young children can practice chanting. In fact, this is recommended, for if a child develops a good chanting routine, then they will surely keep it up for the rest of their life. Chanting the maha-mantra isn't just for Indians either. The name Krishna is God's name, meaning "all-attractive". There is only one God and He is for everyone. Therefore anyone can engage in the process of repeating His name in a loving manner. That is the key. One has to develop a love for God and His name. In fact, this love already exists inside of us, so it is not really a question of developing the love, but more of trying to reawaken it. The love we have for our parents and family members exists naturally, for no one has taught us how to love them. In the same way, our love for Krishna already exists, but it is currently in a dormant state for most of us. Our attachment to fruitive activity has caused us to forget the loving relationship we have with the Lord. Chanting helps us to revitalize it.

All glories to Shri Krishna Chaitanya Mahaprabhu, for giving us the best liquidation sale of all, the free chanting of the Holy name. Let us all take advantage of this great bargain.

Women of the Vedic Tradition

"May Indra protect you on the East, may Yama protect you on the South and Varuna on the West and Kuvera on the North." (Sita Devi speaking to Lord Rama, Valmiki Ramayana, Ayodhya Kand, 16.24)

Women born and raised in the Vedic tradition are perfect in all respects. They maintain the family's traditions and dedication to dharma, or religion. They are the backbone of the family.

According to the Vedas, women and shudras (laborer class) are considered unintelligent. This is due to the fact that traditionally, women and shudras did not receive training from a guru or spiritual master. Though they never received a formal education, some of the greatest devotees of the Lord have been women. Women such as Sita Devi, Savitri, Draupadi, Queen Kunti, and Mother Yashoda were all perfect devotees, whose knowledge and wisdom were on par or exceeded that of great brahmanas and yogis.

In the modern age, the majority of society is considered unintelligent since almost no one receives formal training from a bona fide guru. Most of us attend secular schools where religion isn't discussed due to the concept of "separation of church and state". This presents a challenge to those who want to raise God conscious children. All hope is not lost however, as Vedic principles can still be taught in the home. Though women in the Vedic tradition didn't start attending school until recently, they have always been trained at home by their parents to have a lifestyle based on *tapasya*, or religious austerities. Austerities performed for material benefit doesn't qualify as *tapasya*. One can suffer all they want to, but if that suffering doesn't bring them closer to God, then it is essentially useless. From their very childhood, just like the men, women in the Vedic tradition are taught to fast regularly, properly show respect to the various demigods, and to worship the Supreme Lord, Shri Krishna, or one of His authorized forms. The result is that when girls reach a suitable age for marriage, they are ready to serve their husbands and keep them in check at the same time. Once married, a husband and wife both share the same fate, so it is in the best interests of the wife to make sure the husband is properly observing worship of Krishna. As we all know, sometimes a husband can get out of line and get distracted from the real mission of life, so it is the duty of the wife to not hesitate in pointing out her husband's flaws.

Lord Rama, the incarnation of God in the Treta Yuga, was set to be installed as the new king of Ayodhya by His father Maharaja Dashratha. A messenger had come to the Lord's palace informing Him that He was urgently needed at the king's palace. Taking permission from His wife Sita, the Lord was about leave. Prior to being sent off, she prayed that the various demigods would protect the Lord from all sides. The demigods are each in charge of a specific aspect of the material world, so Sita requested them to give protection to her husband. Lord Rama was God Himself, and He was in no need of any help from anyone, but Sita's request was a sign of her being a good wife. for her mind was always focused on the welfare of her *pati* (husband or master).

In the Vedic tradition, this sort of concern is not only shown towards husbands but to children as well. When Lord Krishna appeared on earth some five thousand years ago, He accepted Yashoda as His foster mother during His childhood years in Vrindavana. The ruler of Mathura at the time, Kamsa, was very worried about suffering death at the hands of Krishna as had been prophesized, so he sent several demons to Vrindavana to kill the young child. As each one came, so they met death at the hands of baby Krishna. The people of Vrindavana were unaware of Krishna's divinity, so they were astonished to see Him survive these attacks from the demons. Mother Yashoda was especially worried about her child. She would regularly recite prayers asking for protection for Krishna. After one incident where baby Krishna survived an attack from the demon Putana, Yashoda and the other gopis (cowherd girls) offered the following prayers:

"'My dear Krishna, may the Lord who is known as Maniman protect Your thighs; may Lord Vishnu who is known as Yajna protect Your legs; may Lord Achyuta protect Your arms; may Lord Hayagriva protect Your abdomen; may Lord Keshava protect Your heart; may Lord Vishnu protect Your arms; may Lord Urukrama protect Your face; may Lord Ishvara protect Your head; may Lord Cakradhara protect Your front; may Lord Gadadhara protect Your back; may Lord Madhusudana who carries a bow in His hand protect Your eyesight; may Lord Vishnu with His conchshell protect Your left side; may the Personality of Godhead Upendra protect You from above, and may Lord Tarkshya protect You from below the earth; may Lord Haladhara protect You from all sides; may the Personality of Godhead known as Hrishikesha protect all Your senses; may Lord Narayana protect Your breath; and may the Lord of Shvetadvipa, Narayana, protect Your heart; may Lord Yogeshvara protect Your mind; may Lord Prishnigarbha protect Your intelligence, and may the Supreme Personality of Godhead protect Your soul. While You are playing, may Lord Govinda protect You from all sides, and when You are sleeping, may Lord Madhava protect You from all danger; when You are working may the Lord of Vaikuntha protect You from falling down; when You are sitting, may the Lord of Vaikuntha give You all protection; and while You are eating, may the Lord of all sacrifices give You all protection.' Thus mother Yashoda began to chant different names of Vishnu to protect the child Krishna's different bodily parts." (Shrila Prabhupada, Krsna, The Supreme Personality of Godhead, Vol 1, Ch 6)

As part of His childhood pastimes, Lord Krishna would go out and play with His cowherd friends. Mother Yashoda would call Krishna and Balarama, His elder brother, home to come eat. She would then feed Them sumptuously, as she was worried Her boys weren't eating enough. "They need their strength." she thought. After the meal, she would lay Them down to rest and give Them betel nuts to chew on as They fell asleep. In this way, she was the perfect mother.

Just like Sita Devi, Yashoda was a perfect woman borne of the Vedic tradition. We still see similar behavior from women in Hindu and Krishna conscious families. Mothers are always nagging their children to eat more. They offer prayers daily for their children's welfare. Prior to leaving for a journey, women will supply the travelers a yogurt mixture as way of guaranteeing a safe journey. Based on historical evidence from the Vedas, we can understand that these traditions have existed for thousands of years. Adherence to these traditions and customs ensures that society will be filled with outstanding citizens. Sita Devi showed her devotion not only the day of Rama's proposed installation, but throughout their marriage. She followed Rama to the forest to serve His exile period alongside Him. While travelling in the woods, she would regularly pray to the Ganges River to protect her husband and ensure that He would survive the fourteen years of exile.

Even today in most Hindu households, it is usually the wives who are more religious, making sure that *arati* of the Lord is performed morning and night, that prasadam is offered and distributed, and that the family members regularly visit temples. All glories to Vaishnava women! May we all learn from their example on how to properly care for our loved ones. Any family which focuses their lives around Krishna and the Vedic traditions will always be guaranteed protection from all sides by the Lord Himself.

The Flag of Devotion

"The emblem of Hanuman on the flag of Arjuna is another sign of victory because Hanuman cooperated with Lord Rama in the battle between Rama and Ravana, and Lord Rama emerged victorious. Now both Rama and Hanuman were present on the chariot of Arjuna to help him. Lord Krishna is Rama Himself, and wherever Lord Rama is, His eternal servitor Hanuman and His eternal consort Sita, the goddess of fortune, are present. Therefore, Arjuna had no cause to fear any enemies whatsoever." (Shrila Prabhupada, BG 1.20 Purport)

We find that in our material endeavors, we often invoke the name or memory of someone as a way of bringing good luck. Athletes often carry good luck charms given to them by legendary figures in their sport. They also remember the accomplishments of previous great athletes prior to having to perform. Politicians will often invoke the names of great leaders from the past when making an important speech.

These are all ways that we try to ensure success in our ventures. When entering a new field or starting a new task, it is best to consult those who have previously been able to triumph. The successful have the necessary experience and wisdom to help us achieve victory since they have gone through similar challenges. In the same way, in order to be successful in spiritual life, we must consult great devotees of the past.

To the normal person, Arjuna's task prior to the start of the Kurukshetra War seemed to be that of a warrior trying to achieve victory for his side. In actuality, since he was following the direct orders of Lord Krishna, the Supreme Personality of Godhead, his task was actually that of performing devotional service to God. Because of this, Arjuna's chariot was decorated with a flag bearing the emblem of Lord Hanuman.

In Lord Krishna's previous incarnation as Lord Rama, there was a great demon named Ravana who had kidnapped Lord Rama's wife, Sita. Hanuman, a Vanara (human-like monkey) and great devotee of Lord Rama, carried out the orders of the Lord and helped defeat Ravana and rescue Sita. Since Arjuna was also involved in a similar task of performing devotional service to the Lord, he made sure to invoke the memory of Krishna's great devotee, Hanuman. In our normal everyday affairs, we tend to forget things that we do, services that we provide for people, and the things that others have done for us. God, on the other hand, never forgets service performed for Him. Hanuman was a pure devotee and helped the Lord, and Krishna never forgot it. He made sure that Hanuman would always be famous as a great devotee. He made sure the name of Hanuman would be synonymous with victory in devotional service.

So the lesson is that we should always remember the great devotees of the Lord and ask them for their mercy in helping us serve Krishna. Arjuna already had God acting as his charioteer, so he had no cause for concern. However, simply by remembering Hanuman, his success was guaranteed. This is God's promise to us. By always remembering Krishna's great devotees and following the example they set forth, we will never meet defeat in our devotional service to the Lord.

Ideal Leadership

"People in general always require a leader who can teach the public by practical behavior. A leader cannot teach the public to stop smoking if he himself smokes. Lord Chaitanya said that a teacher should behave properly even before he begins teaching. One who teaches in that way is called acharya, or the ideal teacher. Therefore, a teacher must follow the principles of shashtra (scripture) to reach the common man." (Shrila Prabhupada, Bhagavad-gita 3.21 Purport)

U.S. President Barrack Obama recently signed legislation aimed at curbing the consumption of cigarettes. By allowing the Food and Drug Administration (FDA) to have enhanced power in regulating tobacco companies, and the products they produce and sell, proponents of the legislation hope that less people will take to smoking as a result. Though he has been a smoker all his adult life, who may or may not have quit recently, President Obama said the new legislation was necessary due to his belief that tobacco companies were actively recruiting young adults to take up smoking:

"Kids today don't just start smoking for no reason. They're aggressively targeted as customers by the tobacco industry. They're exposed to a constant and insidious barrage of advertising where they live, where they learn, and where they play. Most insidiously, they are offered products with flavorings that mask the taste of tobacco and make it even more tempting."

Anyone who has been around smokers for any length of time, knows that smoking is a very nasty habit. Second-hand smoke and the smell that cigarettes leave aren't very pleasing to smokers and to those around them. Aside from having many health risks associated with it, the act of smoking is a form of intoxication which is one of the four pillars of sinful life (intoxication, gambling, illicit sex life, and meat eating).

Intoxication is considered sinful not only for the negative karma associated with it, but also because it causes one to become bound up in material life. If one is attached to material pleasures, then God kindly facilitates by allowing that person to repeatedly take birth in the material world, whereby they are given ample opportunity for sense gratification. Thus the cycle of karma perpetually repeats, since one's senses can never become completely satisfied. It is not until after having lived many lives that one becomes aware of this situation.

"After many births and deaths, he who is actually in knowledge surrenders unto Me, knowing Me to be the cause of all causes and all that is. Such a great soul is very rare." (Lord Krishna, Bhagavad-gita 7.19)

For the past twenty years or so, there has been concerted attack mounted against the tobacco industry. Not wanting to take responsibility for their actions, disgruntled smokers have banded together with lawyers to blame tobacco companies for the harmful side effects of smoking. After winning billions of dollars in lawsuits and levying excessive taxes on tobacco, anti-smoking leaders have failed to get people to quit smoking. In the state of New York, a single pack of cigarettes can cost upwards of $9, yet people still are willing to buy them. The addiction to nicotine is so strong, that the President himself may still smoke, though he has tried to quit many times.

Any attempt made to limit the practice of intoxication is surely a noble one, but such attempts will never be successful unless the leaders themselves adhere to the same restrictions. According to Vedic principles, a leader should lead not only lead by word, but by example as well. Kings of the past would always take counsel from brahmanas, the priests of society. Even if they themselves weren't well versed in the proper code of conduct, they would unhesitatingly abide by the counsel of the brahmanas. In modern society, such a system doesn't exist. The shudras, those unfamiliar with any religious tenets, serve as leaders, while true brahmanas are almost impossible to find. A leader must be very pious, for the other citizens will naturally follow his lead. A president is on television all the time, with the press corps following and recording his every move. Whether they like it or not, the president and other world leaders serve as role models for the rest of society since they are constantly in the public eye.

Not just President Obama, but most leaders in society suffer from the same defects. This is the sign of Kali Yuga, the age of quarrel and hypocrisy where dharma exists at only one fourth its original strength. Leaders preach one thing to their subjects, while they act in totally the opposite way. Government leaders are constantly telling people that they need to sacrifice for the common good and that it's only fair that they, the citizens, give upwards of fifty percent of their income to the government. In the meantime, Senators and other politicians in high offices are some of the wealthiest people in the country, not sacrificing anything for anyone. People are very in tune with this reality. Knowing that their leaders aren't very pious, they feel free to act sinfully themselves.

It is most important to have leaders who adhere strictly to the laws of dharma as enjoined in the shashtras, or authoritative scriptures. Lord Rama was one such leader. An incarnation of Lord Krishna, the Supreme Personality of Godhead, Lord Rama served as the king of Ayodhya, one in a long line of highly respected kings known collectively as the Ikshvaku Dynasty. Lord Rama was completely dedicated to dharma, and was the ultimate renunciate. He never asked His citizens to do something that He Himself wasn't willing to do. He spent fourteen years as an exile in the forest, surviving on fruits and roots, simply to maintain the good name of His father. Towards the end of His life, He renounced His wife Sita, the purest and kindest woman who ever lived, simply to show favor to a citizen who had complained about the Lord's behavior. The citizens were well aware of the Lord's dedication to them and for this reason Lord Rama enjoyed universal love and adoration. The ideal society that existed during His reign was known as Rama Rajya, and many today hearken for a return to it.

In the Vedic system, the government is to be run by the warrior class of men, known as kshatriyas. The government's job is to protect its citizens and administer justice fairly and equally, so brave and pious warriors are required. In today's society, the system is quite different, where leaders are elected directly by the people. Since elections are essentially popularity contests, leaders are elected based on their speaking and arguing abilities verses their capacity to provide protection to their citizens. As a result, today's governments consist mostly of lawyers instead of military men. All hope is not lost however. Instead of dharma trickling down from the top, it can be introduced at the grassroots level first. If enough of the voting population becomes Krishna, or God conscious, then inevitably some of them will run for political office and hopefully win. In this way, with pure devotees serving in government, we can hopefully return to the days of Rama Rajya. In such a situation, everyone will easily be able to break all their bad habits, including smoking.

Better Than a Superhero

"O Sita, there is none who can defeat your husband. There is not the least doubt in this. Worshipful madam, the celestials, animals, birds, and others...there is none among them who can withstand Rama, who equals the lord of celestials, Indra, in warfare. In fact there is none who can do away with Rama in battle." (Lakshmana speaking to Sita Devi, Valmiki Ramayana, Aranya Kand, Sec 45)

The latest *Batman* movie to be released, *The Dark Night*, set records for box office attendance. Based on the fictional superhero character of the same name, previous *Batman* movies also enjoyed similar successes with movie goers. The *Star Wars* and *Lord of the Rings* movies were so popular that they spawned multiple sequels. The *Spiderman* movies are another popular series. It seems the best way to ensure a box office hit these days is to come out with a fantasy movie involving one or more superheroes.

The *Star Wars* movies hold their own unique place in our culture. The first movie, released in 1976, was so popular that people eagerly anticipated the five movies that followed over the next thirty plus years. Fans would camp out in movie theater parking lots just so they could be the first ones to see the new movies. Others would dress up as their favorite characters as a sign of loyalty and adoration. Fans would go back to the theaters to see the same movie two and three times. They just couldn't get enough.

The popularity of these and other movies involving superheroes shows our natural affinity towards strength and courage. We like to see the good guys win. We understand that we are mere mortals and have limited abilities, so we are drawn to those who can rise above the limitations of ordinary human beings. Superheroes have extraordinary powers that enable them to defeat enemies of immense strength. Movies like *Spiderman*, *Superman*, and *Batman* show ordinary people doing extraordinary things through their special powers. The heroes struggle through adversity, but never give up, and always win in the end. We see evil all around us in our daily lives and we feel helpless in stopping it. Superheroes give us hope that maybe someone is out there who can protect us and give us peace of mind.

Though these stories are very nice and uplifting, they are nonetheless fictional. They were drawn up by the imagination of writers and comic book creators. Once the movie ends, we go back to our normal lives, where superheroes don't exist. All hope is not lost however.

Many thousands of years ago, there was a great demon by the name of Ravana who was wreaking havoc throughout the world. He had performed many great austerities in order to please the demigods and they rewarded him with special powers. According to the Vedas, the ancient scriptures of India, the demigods are elevated living entities who manage the affairs of the material world. They are not God, but they have been deputed by Him to handle different departments relating to karmic activity, similar to the way a President will have a variety of Cabinet secretaries handling specific areas of government. The demigods grant benedictions to pretty much anyone who pleases them to their satisfaction. In Ravana's case, He was given ten heads and granted the boon that no demigod, celestial being, or animal could defeat him. Lost in the jubilation of his new found powers, Ravana forgot to ask to be immune from human beings. Ravana belonged to the Rakshasa race, people who lived off eating flesh and drinking wine. He was an enemy to devotees of God and he persecuted them every chance he could get. Ravana steadily rose to power as a result of the boons he received. The demigods were all afraid of him, as were the great sages, or brahmanas, living in the forests.

Lord Vishnu, God Himself, was informed of the situation by the demigods. To relieve their stressful situation and give protection to the sages, He decided to incarnate on earth as a human being in the form of Lord Rama. He appeared as an ordinary human being, who was the kindest, nicest, most courageous, and the most dedicated to dharma, or righteousness, of all people. He had no desire to please Himself in any way. He was completely dedicated to those who were dependent on Him. The name *Rama* actually means "one who gives pleasure". At the request of His father, the king of Ayodhya, and step-mother, the Lord spent fourteen years as an exile from His kingdom. His wife Sita and younger brother Lakshmana insisted on accompanying Him to the forest, for they didn't want the Lord to suffer alone. God actually never suffers, but since He was playing the role of a human being, He agreed to put Himself into stressful situations for the benefit of others. One day while they were living in the forest, a demon by the name of Marica appeared in front of their cottage in the guise of a deer. Sita was very much enamored by the deer and requested Rama to catch it for her, with its life in tact if possible. The Lord chased the demon a long way, finally piercing it with an arrow. As Marica gave up his life, he revealed his original Rakshasa form, and cried out for help in the voice of Rama. Sita, hearing this and getting worried, told Lakshmana to see if Rama was alright. In response, Lakshmana, in the above referenced quote, reminded her that Rama was unconquerable in battle and that the sound must have been an illusion. Nevertheless, as events played out, Lakshmana would end up leaving Sita's side to go check on His brother, which gave Ravana the opportunity to kidnap Sita and take her to his palace.

Already an exile ranging the forest, now the Lord had to deal with the abduction of His most beautiful and chaste wife. Rama persevered and with the help of the Vanaras, monkey-like people dwelling in the forest, He was able to defeat Ravana in battle and rescue Sita, proving Lakshmana's words to be true.

We needn't look to movies or comic books to find a superhero. Lord Rama is the ultimate protector, with powers greater than those of any fictional character. God comes to this earth from time to time specifically so we can have someone to look up to and worship. In times of trouble, we need only turn to Him, as He is the most powerful and most courageous. The lessons from Lord Rama's story are timeless. The *Star Wars* movies depicted material advancement in the modes of warfare. Even with advanced weaponry, Darth Vader's empire was defeated by the powers of good, represented by the Jedis. Similarly, Ravana's great powers achieved through great boons were no match for Rama's army, consisting of monkeys hurling rocks and trees. The monkeys, headed by Rama's greatest devotee Hanuman, were fighting for the good guys, with God on their side, so their victory was guaranteed. Ravana's demon army cast many illusory spells and used trickery as their weapons. Lord Rama and His brother Lakshmana used simple bows and arrows to defeat them. That is the power of God. He can turn a simple arrow into something more powerful than the strongest nuclear weapon.

God is eternal and so are His various forms. Lord Rama's activities are still celebrated to this day in India and throughout the world. We are eternally indebted to Maharishi Valmiki and Goswami Tulsidas for giving us the story of the Lord in such great detail. We should all read the Valmiki Ramayana or Ramacharitamanasa at least once in our lives. The story is so wonderful and moving, that we'll never get tired of reading it. Though the actual events occurred many thousands of years ago, through the power of His holy name, Lord Rama is still with us, helping us fight the Ravanas of today. Let us always remember the Lord, chant His name, and offer Him our prayers. By so doing, our lives will become perfect.

Flying High

"A pure devotee is constantly engaged-sometimes he chants, sometimes he hears or reads books about Krishna, or sometimes he cooks prasadam or goes to the marketplace to purchase something for Krishna, or sometimes he washes the temple or the dishes-whatever he does, he does not let a single moment pass without devoting his activities to Krishna Such action is in full *samadhi*." (Shrila Prabhupada, Bhagavad-gita, 12.2 Purport)

The purchase of a new motorcycle is one of the more obvious indications of someone in the midst of a midlife crisis. Reaching the halfway point of one's life means that one has endured life's ups and downs. After successfully starting and raising a family, along with maintaining a steady job, people reach a point where they want more out of life. Something is lacking; there is a spark that is missing.

Often times, people going through such a period will make an impulse purchase and buy a brand new motorcycle or high end sports car. Fast cars and motorcycles are the ultimate symbols of freedom and adventure. Since they can travel at such high speeds, they are much more dangerous than a regular automobile. To operate them properly, one must give their full attention at all times. There is a natural thrill built into operating one of these vehicles. Being on the the open road, you feel liberated, with nothing keeping you down...just you and the road ahead.

Similar to the exhilaration and euphoria felt from driving fast cars, religion also brings liberation and bliss, except on a much higher level. According to the Vedas, our souls have been bound up in the repeated cycle of birth and death in this material world. We can only be released from this cycle through devotional service to God. Though religion often has a negative and restrictive stigma attached to it, it is actually meant to be just the opposite. If we lovingly devote ourselves to God, then we will feel complete freedom from all material miseries. We are suffering in this life because we are falsely identifying with our material bodies. We think that sense gratification is the be-all end-all when in fact, we see from experience that our senses are never satisfied.

People generally buy a motorcycle or a fancy sports car because they feel a void in their life. That void is actually a spiritual one, and not a material one. No material possession will fill that void. The only way to make ourselves truly happy is to engage our senses in spiritual activities. Following religious principles actually leads one to the path of liberation. Driving a motorcycle may bring about feelings of liberation, but that experience is temporary. In fact, everything associated with the material world is temporary. There are many philosophers who take the creation and the people in it to be false, so they try to just block everything out through meditation. They sit in a secluded place concentrating on nothingness, in hopes of reaching the stage known as nirvana, where everything material is negated.

In the Vedic system, we are taught that this world is in fact real, but temporary. We cannot block out material impediments through artificial means such as impersonal meditation. Instead, we are told to concentrate our minds on the Supreme Lord Krishna, and dovetail all our activities in His service. Through this process, we can achieve *samadhi* or complete concentration of the mind on Krishna, even while performing acts which appear to be material.

The life and times of Lord Hanuman is a great example that illustrates this point. Lord Rama was the incarnation of Krishna who appeared many thousands of years ago in India. Born into a family of *kshatriya* kings, the Lord was the best of fighters. Through a series of unfortunate events, He was forced into exile by His father, who was the king of Ayodhya at the time. While serving His term in the forest, His wife Sita, who had accompanied Him, was kidnapped by the Rakshasa demon Ravana. Lord Rama couldn't go back to Ayodhya and get His army since that would violate His father's order. Instead, he enlisted the help of Vanaras, a race of monkeys with human-like characteristics.

Among the Vanaras, Hanuman is the greatest warrior, with tremendous strength and powers. He is the son of the wind God, Vayu, so he naturally inherits all the strength of the wind. According to Vedic philosophy, air or wind is the strongest element since it represents the vital sign of life. As long as one has air in the body, they are alive and able to function. It is the air inside the body that provides strength. For this reason, people striving for perfection in *ashtanga-yoga* are taught to control the vital life force through the practice of *pranayama*, which involves various breathing exercises. The real purpose of *pranayama* is to prevent the mind and senses from engaging in fruitive activity, or any acts not relating to Krishna's service.

Hanuman has extraordinary strength, but he uses it only for good and not evil. He is Rama's greatest devotee from birth, so he immediately surrendered unto Him when the Lord needed help in rescuing Sita and defeating Ravana. Hanuman is famously depicted travelling to the island of Lanka by flying through the air at the speed of the wind. Ravana's kingdom was in Lanka, and it was also where Sita was held captive. Hanuman bravely went there to deliver to her a message from Rama. He met many obstacles along his way and also while in Lanka, but he never wavered from his duty. He was completely liberated throughout the entire process, though it appeared he was involved in material activities. This was all due to his devotion and pure love for Rama. One who loves God and serves Him sincerely will always feel free and happy. They don't require a fast car, motorcycle, or expertise in *pranayama* to feel happiness, for just the thought of Rama and His pleasing smile fills their hearts with joy.

Cause for Celebration

Elegant dinners, lavish spending, and nights out on the town are all different ways of having a good time. We all like to treat ourselves every now and then. A night out at an expensive restaurant is a great way to celebrate a special occasion. We gather all our family and friends together, and spare no expense in the celebration. Fifty dollars steaks, hundred dollar bottles of wine, and savory soufflés are the staples of fine dining in America.

Consuming food is necessary in order to properly maintain the body and satisfy hunger pains. Regular food items, such as vegetables, grains, and milk, are relatively inexpensive. Yet for special occasions, we don't mind spend a little extra on something that normally doesn't cost much. We like to have fun, and going out to expensive restaurants is exciting and it gives us something to look forward to at the same time.

Devotees of Lord Krishna similarly like to have lavish celebrations. It is a misconception that religious people don't know how to have fun. In fact the Vedas advise us specifically to become servants of the Supreme Lord and that such service will be more fun than any ordinary material activity. Being religious doesn't mean that we have to sit in quiet meditation and renounce all our activities. On the contrary, the highest form of religion is referred to as devotional service, which is full of action and excitement. Serving God means satisfying our spiritual senses and having more fun than a human being should be allowed to have. Since the Lord has appeared on earth many times in different incarnations, devotees use the calendar year to celebrate specific pastimes that the Lord performed during His time here. Couples very much in love often celebrate many different occasions and anniversaries aside from the standard Valentine's Day and birthdays. Most married couples have a celebration each year on the calendar day of their wedding. However, newly formed couples might celebrate each month or each week on the day that they formally became a couple. They essentially look for any opportunity they can get to celebrate their love and affection for each others.

In a similar manner, devotees look for any opportunity they can get to celebrate a particular activity or appearance of Lord Krishna. The Lord specifically gave us these holidays so that we could have fun serving and remembering Him. Festivals likes Krishna's birthday, Janmashtami, are celebrated with great pomp around the world. Devotees spend lavishly to decorate temples and their homes. Expensive flowers are purchased and offered to the Lord. Devotees gather around to sing songs and read stories about Krishna and His pastimes. Elaborate food preparations are made and offered to the Lord. Devotees fast and remain awake until midnight so that they can celebrate the exact time that the Lord appeared from the womb of Mother Devaki. The Lord's appearance occurred around five thousand years ago in the town of Mathura, and it was under trying circumstances. Devaki and her husband Vasudeva were prisoners of King Kamsa, who was Devaki's brother. On the day of their wedding, a voice from the sky informed Kamsa that his death would come at the hands of the eighth son of Devaki and Vasudeva. For this reason, he locked up both Devaki and her husband, and killed each of their first seven sons. Krishna's appearance was a cause for celebration, not only because He was God, but because His appearance signaled the end of the couple's suffering since He was to kill Kamsa.

When Lord Krishna advented on this earth and was growing up in Vrindavana, He specifically instituted a great festival Himself, known as Govardhana Puja. Krishna's foster father, Nanda Maharaja, regularly performed puja, or worship, to the demigod Indra. Lord Krishna convinced him to have a puja for Govardhana Hill instead. His specific instructions were,

"Prepare very nice foodstuffs of all descriptions from the grains and ghee collected for the yajna. Prepare rice, dahl, then halavah,

pakora, puri and all kinds of milk preparations like sweet rice, sweetballs, sandesha, rasagulla and ladoo and invite the learned brahmanas who can chant the Vedic hymns and offer oblations to the fire. The brahmanas should be given all kinds of grains in charity. Then decorate all the cows and feed them well. After performing this, give money in charity to the brahmanas. As far as the lower animals are concerned, such as the dogs, and the lower grades of people, such as the candalas, or the fifth class of men who are considered untouchable, they also may be given sumptuous prasadam. After giving nice grasses to the cows, the sacrifice known as Govardhana Puja may immediately begin. This sacrifice will very much satisfy Me." (Krishna, The Supreme Personality of Godhead, Ch 24)

Govardhana Puja was subsequently performed, and it has been a tradition ever since. It was due to Lord Krishna's kindness that He gave us this and many other wonderful festivals to celebrate. So let us spare no expense is glorifying the Lord. The Christmas Holiday is very nice, but why not dedicate every day to God? Living by this principle will make us happy and joyful throughout the year. The Lord has innumerable pastimes that we can celebrate, so there is always something to look forward to. By celebrating in this way, we purify ourselves and have fun doing it. We get the same thrills and excitement as having an elegant night out on the town, with all the spiritual benefits included.

When Violence is Necessary

"According to Vedic injunctions there are six kinds of aggressors: 1) a poison giver, 2) one who sets fire to the house, 3) one who attacks with deadly weapons, 4) one who plunders riches, 5) one who occupies another's land, and 6) one who kidnaps a wife. Such aggressors are at once to be killed, and no sin is incurred by killing such aggressors." (Shrila Prabhupada, Bhagavad-gita As It Is 1.36 Purport)

Question: How can you worship Krishna, who instructed Arjuna to fight in a war that led to the death of millions?

Answer: The ideas of religion and violence never seem to go hand in hand. Religion means to see outside of one's own body and to see the spirit soul in all of us. This naturally removes feelings of lust, greed, and anger, which are the forbearers to violence. Because of this, many mistakenly think violence itself is completely unnecessary and never warranted.

According to the Vedic teachings, violence is not only allowed, but it is required in certain situations. The kshatriyas, or warrior class of people, are required to provide protection to the other members of society. From our experience, we see that not everyone is a good or nice person. Some people are always angry and looking for a fight. Material nature is divided into three qualitative modes, the modes of goodness, passion, and ignorance. People in the mode of ignorance are naturally inclined to be violent towards others since they lack the knowledge required to settle disputes peacefully. The Vedas say that one has a right to defend and protect themselves if attacked by such people.

The circumstances related to the Bharata War provide a great example of when violence is necessary. Around five thousand years ago, two families, known as the Pandavas and the Kauravas, who were related as cousin-brothers, had a disagreement over who had the right to rule over a kingdom. The Pandavas were the sons of Pandu, and the Kauravas were the sons of Dhritarashtra, Pandu's brother. Pandu was a great king who died prematurely due to a curse. His sons were the rightful heirs to the kingdom, but Dhritarashtra favored his sons instead and allowed them to unjustly usurp power over the kingdom. The Pandavas naturally objected to this and the struggle between the two families culminated in the Bharata War, which took place on the battlefield of Kurukshetra in India. Arjuna, the leading warrior for the Pandavas, was getting ready to start fighting, but he suddenly felt faint of heart and didn't want to fight. He started thinking along the lines of nonviolence, and he questioned his cousin about it, Lord Krishna. Their conversation is chronicled in the Bhagavad-gita.

Arjuna's soft-heartedness was very characteristic of a devotee of God. Though they were cousins, Arjuna and Krishna were also great friends growing up, with Arjuna looking up to the Lord. When Krishna appears on earth, He usually doesn't disclose His divinity to most people. If everyone knew He was God, then they might fear Him instead of becoming His friend. Krishna prefers devotional service performed in the mood of friendship and love rather than out of fear. As a devotee, Arjuna possessed all good qualities, with one of them being kindness and benevolence towards all. A devotee is by nature nonviolent, not wanting to hurt even an ant unnecessarily. In his youth, Arjuna and his brothers spent much time with their cousins, the sons of Dhritarashtra. They were all descendants of their great grandfather Bhishma, who was respected by all. They all received training in the military arts from their spiritual master Dronacharya. Now both Dronacharya and Bhishmadeva were on the battlefield, but fighting for the side of the Kauravas. Arjuna did want to engage in a fight against such respectable people. He did want to win a kingdom if it meant killing other family members. These feelings overwhelmed Arjuna, and he decided that he would not fight and instead become a renunciate.

Lord Krishna, the Supreme Personality of Godhead, who was serving as His cousin's charioteer at the time, quickly admonished Arjuna, telling him that his behavior was not worthy of a kshatriya. Kshatriyas make up one of the four *varnas* in the Vedic *varnashrama* dharma system. Their duty is to provide protection to all the citizens, and especially to the brahmanas (priestly class). Krishna told Arjuna that it was his duty to fight. Here we get the definitive judgment on when violence is necessary from God Himself. Violence is necessary when it is done on religious principles. It was Arjuna's religious duty to fight. Lord Krishna tells us that each person should faithfully perform his or her occupational duties in life, without attachment. In this way, there is no sin incurred from even acting violently.

"It is far better to discharge one's prescribed duties, even though they may be faulty, than another's duties. Destruction in the course of performing one's own duty is better than engaging in another's duties, for to follow another's path is dangerous." (Lord Krishna, Bhagavad-gita, 3.55)

Therefore He advised Arjuna to execute the duties of a kshatriya instead of those of a brahmana.

Force is necessary to have peace. Police exist for this very reason. We see in areas where there is not a strong kshatriya presence, that crime is very high and the citizens do not feel safe. Diplomacy has its use, but it usually never brings about lasting peace. In peaceful negotiations, people will say whatever they need to in order to further their position. Lord Krishna Himself tried diplomacy prior to the Bharata War, but He knew that it wouldn't be successful due to the obstinacy of the Kauravas.

War can be very ugly. The Bharata War saw millions of soldiers die. Yet violence as a last resort, performed on religious principles is a necessary evil in life. Nonviolence is a very nice concept in theory, but not always practical. Even brahmanas, who are taught to be nonviolent, defend themselves when necessary. The great sage Vashishta procured various weapons to defend himself from the attacks of Vishwamitra Muni, who was trying to steal Vashishta's cow.

In the end, the best way to achieve everlasting peace is for everyone to be constantly engaged in devotional service to the Lord. We can always be thinking of God by reading books about Him, serving His authorized representative, and by always chanting His name. This was the method prescribed by Lord Chaitanya and all the great Vaishnava acharyas. Following their instructions, we can all live peacefully and hopefully never have to fight with anyone.

Mega Memory

"Formerly, before Vyasadeva, say, five thousand years ago, before that time there was no need of written literature. People were so sharp in their memory that whatever they would hear from the spiritual master they would remember for life. The memory was so sharp. But in this age—it is called Kali Yuga—we are reducing our bodily strength, our memory..." (Shrila Prabhupada, Lecture, 790902.VP.NV)

According to the shastras, or Vedic scriptures, the earth doesn't come into being just once, but rather is created and destroyed in repeating cycles. Each creation exists for a fixed time period, which is divided into four ages known as Yugas. The four Yugas are Satya, Treta, Dvapara, and Kali.

Satya Yuga is the first time period beginning at creation. Satya means "truth" so the people living in this age are known for being strictly dedicated to dharma. Dharma means occupational duty or religion, and people abide by it at almost a one hundred percent level in the Satya Yuga. Which each successive Yuga, dharma diminishes in strength by one quarter, thus causing a rise in irreligion. We are currently living in the last Yuga, known as Kali. Kali Yuga is famous for the widespread presence of adharma, or activity which is against the scriptural injunctions. Dharma exists only at one fourth its original strength in the Kali Yuga.

In the classic Vedic system, society is to be managed according to *varnashrama* dharma. There are four *varnas*, or societal divisions based on a people's qualities. The brahmanas are the religious class of people, who are viewed as the highest class members of society. Kshatriyas serve as the warriors and administrators, providing protection to the other three classes of society. Vaishyas are the merchants and businessmen who are entrusted with cow protection, farming, and general economic development. The shudras are the last group, and since they receive no formal training from a spiritual master, their duty is to serve the other three *varnas*. Shudras are traditionally those of the laborer class. Just as there are four *varnas*, there are also four *ashramas*, or stages in one's life. The first *ashrama* is known as *brahmacharya* and it is the time period when one is living a life of complete celibacy and taking instruction from a spiritual master. After completing one's training under a guru, one then enters the *grihastha ashrama*, which is married householder life. Then after twenty five years, one retires from family life and enters the *vanaprastha ashrama*. Finally, the last stage of life is known as *sannyasa*, where one completely renounces all family attachments and material possessions and lives completely at the mercy of God.

In the Kali Yuga, this system is virtually nonexistent. Shudras are praised and held in high regard, while brahmanas are vilified. The most sinful among us serve as our exalted leaders, preaching irreligion as a way of life. We see evidence of this everywhere today, especially with the widespread practices of animal slaughter and abortion. One of the most harmful side effects of Kali Yuga is the overall loss of intelligence and brain power in people. Though we may think that the overall life expectancy is rising, in actuality in previous Yugas the average duration of life was much greater than it is today. This is all a result of overindulgence in sense gratification. When one is constantly hankering after satisfying the needs of the stomach and the genitals, intelligence will be clouded. One is left no time to contemplate the real problems of life, which are birth, old age, disease, and death. When people's lives revolve around eating, sleeping, mating, and defending, then naturally their intelligence will suffer.

One need only look to the advent of the teleprompter to see a glaring example of how the brainpower of man has rapidly declined. Used by everyone from politicians to television reporters, the teleprompter is a device that provides an electronic visual of the text of a speech given by a speaker. With a teleprompter, one isn't required to commit a speech to memory. One need only focus their attention on the device while making a speech, for the prompter will scroll through the text at the speaker's pace, guaranteeing that the speaker will never forget what to say next. Teleprompters are positioned in such a way that the audience usually can't tell that the speaker is using it. For speeches that are delivered to television audiences, the prompter is usually aligned with the television camera, so the speaker can read the text of the speech while pretending to look directly at the audience watching on their televisions at home.

There is nothing necessarily wrong with teleprompters, since they allow for the smooth delivery of speeches. However, what has happened is that speakers have become lazy as a result of using them. One doesn't even have to be familiar with the subjects they are talking about since they can just read whatever is put in front of them. As recently as twenty years ago, speakers at least had to memorize the speeches they gave, thus allowing the subject matter to be retained in their minds where it could be processed and pondered over. Today, many speakers, including the President of the United States, have committed embarrassing blunders such as reading the wrong speech or talking out of order due to malfunctions with the teleprompters. There are many world leaders who are great at delivering speeches, but when asked questions on policy in interviews, they stutter and stammer due to lack of knowledge on the subjects they are being questioned on.

In previous Yugas, people's brains were so sharp that they could memorize millions of Sanskrit verses after only hearing them once. The great Maharishi Valmiki committed the entire Ramayana to memory and would recite it perfectly to others. He even taught it to Lord Rama's two sons, Lava and Kusha, who would regularly recite it in front of gathered assemblies in their father's kingdom. Vyasadeva, Lord Krishna's literary incarnation, authored eighteen Puranas, the Vedanta-sutras, and the Mahabharata all from memory. The

Mahabharata itself is probably the longest book ever written so it is amazing to think that one man could commit that entire work to memory. But it wasn't only Vyasadeva, for he had many disciples who also became expert orators. The Shrimad Bhagavatam, also known as the Bhagavata Purana, was recited by Shukadeva Goswami, Vyasadeva's son. These people were all exalted brahmanas, who had dedicated their lives to serving Krishna, or God. Their intelligence was top notch as a result. These sages didn't limit themselves to just memorization, for they had a deep understanding of the topics and stories they would recite.

There is no denying that Kali Yuga is in full force, with its effects seen everywhere. Obviously it is not possible for people to commit such great works to memory anymore. Luckily for us, all hope is not lost. In this age, all the wisdom of the Vedas has been summarized into one short phrase, the maha-mantra:

"Hare Krishna Hare Krishna, Krishna Krishna, Hare Hare, Hare Rama Hare Rama, Rama Rama, Hare Hare"

Krishna and Rama are names of God, and Hare is His energy. There is no knowledge or truth higher than God. Committing this mantra to memory and regularly reciting it in the presence of others will make us the greatest of orators.

The Perfect Marriage

83

"Then bringing the beautifully ornamented Sita near the fire and placing her before Lord Rama, Maharaja Janaka spoke to Rama and said, 'Take this, my daughter Sita, as your partner in the observance of all duties, and do take her hand and place it by yours. May she always be pious and devoted to you, and always follow you like your own shadow.' (Valmiki Ramayana, Bala Kanda, Sec 73)

When Lord Krishna incarnated on earth as Lord Rama, He accepted the goddess of fortune herself, Sita Devi as His wife. Sita was the daughter of the extremely pious King Janaka of Mithila. On a previous occasion, Janaka had been given a sacred bow of Lord Shiva. Since he held both the bow and his daughter in high regard, Janaka decided that whoever would be able to lift and string the bow would win Sita's hand in marriage. At the occasion of Sita's *svayamvara* (ceremony where a groom is chosen from a list of eligible suitors), Lord Rama not only lifted the bow, but He broke it as well. In this way, He won Sita's hand in marriage.

Like most Vedic sacrifices, a marriage ceremony takes place in the presence of a fire. In the above referenced verse, King Janaka is asking Rama to accept Sita as His wife, and wishing for his daughter to be forever devoted to her husband. In doing so, Janaka here is describing the dharma, or religious duties, of a wife in marriage. The Vedas tell us that the prime duty of a wife is for her to faithfully serve her husband. The husband in turn is to provide complete protection for his wife. This way, the couple can live happily and peacefully, each equally adhering to their prescribed duties. Modern day society likes to preach the equality of men and women, and how marriages should be fifty-fifty partnerships built on compromise and give and take. Technically, they are correct in one sense since the husband and wife are both equal on a spiritual level. The most important Vedic tenet is that we are not our bodies. We are spirit souls at our core. All living entities are equal in their constitutional position. As far as a marriage goes, the husband and wife both share the same spiritual fate, so they are equal in that sense. A marriage is a partnership in that the husband and wife should both equally perform the specific duties prescribed for them. In this way, they will be happy in marriage and have time to focus on the real aim of life, serving God.

Many people misconstrue the meaning behind the Vedic tenet that a wife should serve her husband. They view this as a sort of slavery system, but it is not so. Vedic life is centered around the idea of God realization. The human form of life is very auspicious since only human beings have the capacity to understand who is God, and to use that knowledge to break out of the perpetual cycle of birth and death. Thus Vedic prescriptions are all geared to help one achieve this goal. Since the material world is always pulling our senses in every which direction, serving Krishna is a very difficult thing to do. God gave us the institution of marriage so that we would have a partner in our service to Him. There are many specific *samskaras* (rites) and ritualistic performances enjoined in the shastras. Married couples should perform these specific purificatory rites together. From our own experiences, we find that our duties are easier to perform when we have our friends and family helping and supporting us. A good spouse is someone we can count on for support at all times. The Vedas tell us that a devoted wife earns all the religious merits accumulated by her husband, so she elevates herself simply through serving her *pati* or husband.

The Mahabharata tells us that the main occupation of those in the *grihastha ashrama*, householder life, is to feed Krishna by preparing and offering food to Him, and then to take the prasadam and distribute it to guests. Through hospitably serving guests and brahmanas, a married couple becomes purified and elevated in their spiritual consciousness. Householders should always have guests at their home, for they receive tremendous spiritual merit by serving their guests and attending to their every need. In this day and age, especially in the Western countries, most people are accustomed to eating animal flesh and other dirty things. These types of food all have negative karma attached to them. Married couples that are devotees of Krishna have a tremendous opportunity to distribute the mercy of the Lord in the form of His prasadam to people who desperately need it. Prasadam is food that is completely karma free, for Lord Krishna has given His spiritual glance over it and left the remnants for us. Any guest received by a householder should be served this wonderful prasadam, for it is the easiest way to infuse people with spiritual consciousness, giving them the chance to reconnect with the Supreme Lord. There is no higher form of charity than this.

In modern day society where men and women freely interact, the system of marriage has deviated quite a bit from the original system God created. It has become an institution where both the man and women try to love each other, while at the same maintaining their independence. While this may seem like a nice idea, the result is that either the marriage or the independence suffers, both of which lead to unhappiness. The Vedas tell us that there is no concept of independence in a marriage. A woman is to dutifully serve her husband no matter what, and the man is obligated to provide complete protection for his wife. These principles were practiced by the divine couple, Sita Devi and Lord Rama. Sita was completely devoted to Rama in all her thoughts, words, and deeds. She supported Him through thick and thin, even following Him to the forest. Janaka prayed that she would follow Rama like a shadow, and she obliged. Lord Rama, for His part, was equally devoted to her. He was always dedicated to her welfare, even going to great lengths to rescue her when she was kidnapped by the demon Ravana.

From the example set by Sita Devi and Lord Rama, we can learn the proper means to having a happy marriage and a successful life. True love means wanting more for the person you love than you want for yourself. Sita Devi always wished for her Lord to be happy and to always be devoted to Him. Even her father Janaka wished the same for her. This is the true aim of life, to have pure love for God. May we always have the blessings of Sita-Rama in all our endeavors and we may our minds always be concentrated on their lotus feet. The husband and wife who devote themselves to being servants of Sita-Rama, they will enjoy everlasting felicity in this life and the next. They will have the perfect marriage.

God is Nice

"No one is envied by Me, neither am I partial to anyone. I am equal to all; yet whoever renders service unto Me in devotion is a friend, is in Me; and I am a friend to him." (Lord Krishna, Bhagavad-gita 9.29)

We often see God depicted as being very vengeful and someone we should fear. Many of us have passed by the people on the street who sternly warn us to surrender to God or suffer eternal damnation in hell. Natural disasters are viewed by many as God's way of getting revenge on us for our sins. Because of this, many modern organized religions survive by instilling fear in their members. They say that we should fear God and surrender unto Him if we want to be absolved of our sins.

In actuality, God is our dearmost well-wishing friend. Lord Krishna, the Supreme Personality of Godhead according to the Vedic tradition, tells us in the Bhagavad-gita that He is actually neutral to everyone in this material world. This material world was created out of the desire of the spiritual souls to lord over nature. We wanted to pretend to be God, so He granted our wish by allowing us to come to this universe. Due to the influence of *maya*, Krishna's illusory energy, we are all identifying with our bodies and thinking that we are the doer of our activities. We think that the results that we achieve are all due to our own efforts. Deluding ourselves in this way, we spend our lives going further and further away from God.

"The bewildered spirit soul, under the influence of the three modes of material nature, thinks himself to be the doer of activities, which are in actuality carried out by nature." (Lord Krishna, Bhagavad-gita 3.27)

According to the laws of material nature, the living entity is constantly going through the cycle of birth, death, old age, and disease. Due to our work and desires, we accept new bodies after we are finished with our current one. This is the law of karma. We enjoy happiness or suffer through misery due to the karma accumulated in this life and in previous ones. Each individual has their own desires and wants, and the material world is the playing field where the desires of all living entities collide head on with each other. The world stock markets are a good example of this principle in action on a very small scale. On any given day, millions of traders compete with each other to make money through the buying and selling of stocks. Traders all have different temperaments, personalities, and levels of intelligence. Each person has their own goals that they set out to achieve. The trading floor is the arena where all these goals and desires collide and because of this, we see that some people are very successful, while others lose millions and become bankrupt.

These collisions exist in the material world on a much greater level through the three qualities of nature: goodness, passion, and ignorance. Every living entity possesses these qualities in some varying combination. Since not everyone possesses these qualities at the same levels, we see variegations in the species, to the point of 1,400,000 different varieties. Everyone is competing with each other to satisfy their desires, so naturally there will be collisions of varying magnitudes. As a result, from time to time we see horrific tragedies, such as mass murders, terrorist attacks, school shootings, etc. Lord Krishna is not to blame for this, for He is not directly involved with the day to day affairs of the material world.

"As there are constitutional laws in the material world stating that the king can do no wrong, or that the king is not subject to the state laws, similarly the Lord, although He is the creator of this material world, is not affected by the activities of the material world. He creates and remains aloof from the creation, whereas the living entities are entangled in the fruitive results of material activities because of their propensity for lording it over material resources." (Shrila Prabhupada, Bg 4.14 Purport)

Through His energies, this material world was created and through His deputies, the demigods, material affairs are managed. The demigods handle all issues of fairness with regards to karma. God personally has no stake in our material fortunes.

Narasimha killing Hiranyakashipu, Prahlada's father

Lord Krishna makes an exception however when it comes to His devotees. Krishna is very partial towards His devotees and He will do anything to protect them and make them happy. Examples of this affection can be found throughout the historical incidents documented in the great Vedic literatures. In the Treta Yuga, Krishna incarnated as Lord Rama specifically to save His devotees who were being harassed by the demon Ravana. In a previous time, there was a young a boy by the name of Prahlada who was a great devotee of the Lord. Though he was born into the family of the Daityas, who are atheistic by nature, Prahlada was a completely surrendered soul from his very birth. His atheistic father, Hiranyakashipu, very much disliked his son's devotion to God. He tried to kill Prahlada through various means, but Prahlada miraculously survived each and every attack. It was actually no miracle, for the boy simply thought of Lord Krishna during each attack, which is the best way to guarantee one's safety. The Lord always protects His devotees no matter what. Even if they are put into difficult or painful situations, He guarantees that they will return to His abode after quitting their present bodies.

"Anyone who quits his body, at the end of life, remembering Me, attains immediately to My nature; and there is no doubt of this." (Lord Krishna, Bhagavad-gita 8.5)

Finally, the Lord had enough of Hiranyakashipu's deplorable behavior, so He personally incarnated as Narasimha Deva to kill him. This also represents the reverse side of the Lord's favoritism. As kind as He is to His devotees, He is equally unkind to the enemies of His devotees. He will dole out the most severe punishment to the miscreants who dare harm His bhaktas.

This material world is a cause of constant fear. We have so many possessions and relationships that are all destined to end. We try very hard to defend and hold on to these ties, knowing that one day we won't have them. In the spiritual world, such fear doesn't exist. Our relationship with Krishna is eternal, and realizing that relationship means never having to be afraid again. God is not someone that we need to fear. If we learn to love Him, then He will reciprocate times ten. The best way to love God is through the process of bhakti yoga, or devotional service. If we constantly engage ourselves in hearing stories about the Lord, offering Him prayers, and chanting His name, then He will surely notice us. God resides in all of us through His Paramatma, or Supersoul, expansion. By practicing devotional service, we slowly move our consciousness from the material to the spiritual platform, where we can dovetail it with the Supreme Consciousness. Let us all become devotees of Krishna, not out of fear, but out of love for Him and His causeless mercy. He will always love us and never let us down, so we have nothing to fear.

Never Too Late

"...from any stage of life, or from the time of understanding its urgency, one can begin regulating the senses in Krishna consciousness, devotional service of the Lord, and turn the lust into love of Godhead—the highest perfectional stage of human life." (Shrila Prabhupada, Bhagavad-gita, 3.41 Purport)

Drug addiction is a major problem not only in America, but throughout the world. Intoxication is a means of escaping the senses and feeling a false sense of bliss. This feeling is short-lived as the thrill wares off pretty quickly. People are then led to trying other forms of intoxication, each being more and more dangerous.

Drugs like crack, cocaine, marijuana, and even nicotine are all very addictive and have very dangerous side effects. Users become accustomed to the temporary sense pleasure derived by taking such drugs, and thus they become addicts. Drug addiction is a byproduct of the mode of ignorance. The material world is governed by three *gunas* or qualities: goodness, passion, and ignorance. Acts of charity and piety fall under the goodness category, fruitive activity is considered in the mode of passion, and abominable acts that are not conducive to one's spiritual health are considered to be in the mode of ignorance.

"...Such a man appears to be always dejected, and is addicted to intoxicants and sleeping. These are the symptoms of a person conditioned by the mode of ignorance." (Shrila Prabhupada, Bhagavad-gita, 14.8 Purport)

First-time drug users may start out in the mode of passion, but their habit gradually leads them to the mode of ignorance. Most people in the world are living in the mode of passion. Almost everyone is concerned with earning money and seeking sense gratification. We have a craving for something and then we take actions to try to satisfy that craving. However, if those cravings and desires are not controlled, they can lead to feelings of lust. Drug addicts are lusty for their drugs and that lust leads to anger and eventually to bewilderment.

"While contemplating the objects of the senses, a person develops attachment for them, and from such attachment lust develops, and from lust anger arises." (Lord Krishna, Bhagavad-gita 2.62)

People will do anything to get their drugs, even if it includes lying or stealing. Through our own experiences, we know that some of the most skilled liars we have met in life are people who are addicted to drugs. They appear to be very nice and complimentary, but it is all a façade. Accustomed to lying, cheating, and stealing to get their drugs, dishonesty and deceit become their way of life. Their lust is at such a height that they become experts in performing all unrighteous activities.

Devotees of Lord Krishna, on the other hand, are addicted to chanting His glories. Through constantly being associated with God and His bona fide representative, the spiritual master, they naturally become free of all bad habits. The work of His Divine Grace A.C. Bhaktivedanta Swami Prabhupada proved this fact. The founder of the modern day Hare Krishna Movement, Prabhupada came to America in 1965 to teach the true message of the Vedas to the Western world. Though Americans were slow to catch on at first, eventually his movement would steadily gain in popularity, especially amongst the youth. Many of these young boys and girls were former hippies, addicted to dropping acid and smoking marijuana. Prabhupada not only got them to kick their drug habits, but he turned them into bona fide brahmanas or priests. Instead of sleeping through the day, his disciples were trained to wake up very early in the morning, to take a bath and to perform *managala arati* and chanting of the Holy name. They not only gave up their drug habits, but all other forms of intoxication as well. The four pillars of sinful life are meat eating, intoxication, gambling, and illicit sex. Prabhupada's disciples gave up all these habits, and along with their regulated chanting routine, they became first class citizens.

Herein lies the power of the pure devotee of Krishna. Through their example and their dedication to the Lord, they are able to reform anyone. They view every living entity equally, not believing that only certain people are worthy of receiving God's message. The great Narada Muni has also reformed many a great individual. Maharishi Valmiki in his youth was a dacoit by trade, but he gave up that life at the instruction of Narada. He not only gave up his sinful ways, but he turned to glorifying the Lord by composing a poem about Him known as the Ramayana, which become famous throughout the world. This is the grace of the spiritual master. They don't simply ask their disciple to refrain from harmful activities. They instruct them on how to make their lives perfect by taking up the process of devotional service. We may ask someone to stop smoking or drinking, but if after quitting they are still bound in the mode of passion, then we really haven't done anything worthwhile for them. Simply giving people do's and don'ts may be a good thing, but it is not the answer to the real problems of life, namely birth, old age, disease, and death. Charity and benevolence are very nice, but the highest form of charity is to freely distribute love of Godhead. People must be given a higher cause to serve. According to the great acharyas, that cause is the taking up of devotional service to Lord Krishna.

Devotees become expert in telling the truth, in having compassion, and in praising others. These are all righteous qualities that are acquired automatically and without any effort. Simply by connecting with God, one becomes a first class person. Instead of the lust that arises from drug addiction, attachment to God causes spontaneous love to appear in one's heart. Instead of turning to drugs or other intoxicants to satisfy our senses, let us all become addicted to viewing the divine form of the Lord. His name, form, and pastimes are so beautiful that we will continue to be enchanted by them day after day.

The Good Wife

"It is that you speak to me thus, thinking me, no doubt, mean minded. I cannot but laugh at your words." (Sita Devi speaking to Lord Rama, Valmiki Ramayana, Ayodhya Kand Sec 27)

A good wife, who loves her husband very much, is typically found to be very critical of him. A loving wife tends to look at her husband as helpless and not knowing the rules of propriety and proper conduct, similar to the way parents view their children. Because of this love, a wife is never afraid to correct her husband or even to make fun of him if she thinks he is behaving improperly.

Men typically get very annoyed at such behavior from their wives. The idea of the "nagging" wife is very common and it forms the basis of most stereotypical male-female humor. Any opposition from their wives is viewed as nagging. Men love to get together with their friends and tell stories about their wives and how they are constantly haggled by them to clean up their act. Men don't like to be criticized in their choice of clothing, or being told how late they can stay out when hanging out with their friends, or even questioned on the purchases they make. Husbands like to feel in control and like to be supported in their decisions.

Yet in the best of marriages, especially those that have lasted a long time, we see just the opposite situation, where husbands and wives freely and openly argue with each other. In reality, a wife who nags is a wife who loves. When we love someone, we want more for them than we want for ourselves. At the same time, in a loving relationship, there is a strong feeling of attachment and closeness between couples. The more we love someone and the more comfortable we are around them, the more likely we are to be open to criticizing them. If we see a stranger doing something wrong and behaving improperly, we aren't likely to say anything. We think, "Oh I don't know this person. Let them be, I will just mind my own business." Yet if our loved ones act improperly, be it our children, parents, or significant others, we won't hesitate for a moment to correct them. Often misidentified as unnecessary criticism, such interjection is representative of the highest form of love.

Lord Rama, the incarnation of Lord Krishna, the Supreme Personality of Godhead, who appeared on this earth during the Treta Yuga, was all set to be installed as the new king of Ayodhya by His father, Maharaja Dashratha. On the morning of His installation, He was called to His father's royal palace. Leaving His wife Sita Devi at home, Rama speedily repaired to the king's quarters. Upon arriving, He was given the news that the plans had changed, and that Rama's younger brother Bharata was to be installed as the new king instead. This was all due to Dashratha's youngest wife, Kaikeyi, who had called in favors that were due her from the king. Also by her request, Rama was to be exiled from the kingdom and forced to live in the forest for fourteen years. Lord Rama, being God Himself, was the ultimate renunciate, so He had no problem whatsoever with the new plans.

Returning to His palace, Rama informed Sita of the news. While explaining the situation, He also told her not to come with Him to the forest. He warned her about the dangers lurking in the woods and told her that dharma, or religiosity, decreed that she should stay in Ayodhya and serve the elders and the new king. Sita responded by laughing at her husband. Sita Devi was the incarnation of the goddess of fortune, Lakshmi. Lakshmi is always serving Narayana, who is Krishna Himself residing in the spiritual world. So when Lakshmi appeared on this earth as Sita, she was married to Lord Rama and completely dedicated to Him. Being a loving wife, she knew no other truth than Rama. The idea of being separated from her husband seemed outright preposterous. She immediately dismissed this idea just at the mere mention of it. When we feel very strongly about something or someone, we project our feelings onto other people, meaning we find it difficult to imagine that someone else doesn't feel the same way that we do. This applies to foods that we like, our favorite movies, or even to songs that we enjoy. Since our feelings are so strong, we naturally assume people think the same way that we do. Sita loved Rama so much that the idea of being separated from Him made no sense at all. Naturally she assumed that her Lord felt the same way. So when she heard Rama suggesting separation for fourteen years, she naturally laughed at Him. "Why are you being ridiculous? My life is you and only you. You know that! Why are you pretending that you don't know that? Have you lost your mind? There's no way I'm going to live in this kingdom or anywhere else without you." These were the thoughts that went through her mind. A good wife is always the first one to point out her husband's momentary lapses of insanity, so Sita was perfect in this regard. The wife is the better half, and Sita proved it by her devotion to Rama.

Now Lord Rama is flawless so there wasn't actually anything wrong with His suggestion that Sita remain in the kingdom. His love for Sita was equal to her love for Him, and He was just trying to protect her. She was the most beautiful woman in the three worlds, born and raised as a princess. Forest life would be very difficult for anybody, let alone one as lovely as herself. Rama was acting out of pure love by dissuading her from going to the forest. This is the relationship between God and His devotees. The devotees are always thinking of God's interests and God reciprocates. These are the loving exchanges that take place in the spiritual world. We are eternally grateful to Lord Rama and Sita Devi for bringing that same love to this material world, allowing us to take pleasure in their pastimes and learn from their example.

A Time For Charity

"O king, please now proceed to give away cows on behalf of the marriages of Rama and Lakshmana, and performing their ancestral rites, complete the marriage ceremony...On the third day, when the Pahlguna will be on the north, please perform the marriage ceremony my dear king. In the meantime, please proceed in distributing gifts for invoking blessings upon Rama and Lakshmana."

(Janaka speaking to Dashrata prior to the marriage of Lord Rama to Sita Devi, Valmiki Ramayana Bala-Kanda, Sec 71)

When God incarnated as Lord Rama, His marriage was arranged to Sita Devi, the daughter of Maharaja Janaka. A very pious man known for being an expert transcendentalist, Janaka hosted the wedding ceremony and invited Lord Rama's father, Maharaja Dashrata, and members of his kingdom. Janaka was so happy to get Lord Rama as a son in law that he also arranged for Rama's three younger brothers (Bharata, Lakshmana, and Shatrughna) to be married to other members of his royal family. Thus the marriages of all four brothers took place simultaneously.

In the above referenced statement, we see that Janaka is requesting Dashrata to give away cows in charity in order to mark the joyous occasion. All important occasions in Vedic culture are celebrated by giving away cows in charity. When we were children growing up, we always looked forward to our birthdays for we were assured of getting lots of presents. In America, even the Christmas holiday is celebrated this way. People go out and feverishly shop for the perfect gift to give to their loved ones. Children especially love these occasions since they can never have enough toys. In the Vedic tradition, instead of receiving gifts, special occasions are times when we give generously to those in need. This is not just ordinary charity either, for gifts should be given to those who are worthy of them. We may meet a homeless person on the street in need of money, but if they spend the money we give them on drugs and alcohol, then we really haven't done anything for that person. We maybe make ourselves feel better with this type of kindness, but the Vedas tell us that charity should serve a higher purpose than this. According to the Vedas, charity should only be given to brahmanas, or those dedicated to serving Lord Krishna.

When celebrating festive occasions, generally one gives away cows to the brahmanas. Cows are considered to be equal to one's own mother since they freely provide milk to us. Brahmanas generally don't earn a living, so they live off the charity of others. As the priestly class of men, brahmanas dedicate their lives to studying the Vedas and performing sacrifices. Their days are spent preaching the glories of the Lord and counseling the other three *varnas* or divisions of society (kshatriyas, vaishyas, and shudras). A cow is considered a great sign of wealth since it can supply ample amounts of food simply from the milk it provides. The economic problem can be solved simply by maintaining a few cows on one's land.

Weddings in modern society have turned into very stressful affairs. Planning a wedding means deciding on a guest list and making sure it is not too large or too small. Weddings are held in expensive banquet halls so the price per guest is usually very expensive. Halls typically charge the host per head or per person attending, with a minimum number of guests required by the hall. Inviting too many guests means the cost will go up, while too few guests means the hall won't agree to take the wedding. As far as wedding gifts go, the bride and groom-to-be usually register at various retail stores so that guests can pick out items to give as gifts. This ensures that the married couple won't receive the same gifts from multiple people. It is now customary for most guests to give cash gifts at a wedding. According to the standard etiquette as it has evolved, the amount of the gift should be equal to or greater than the cost incurred by the host to allow that guest to come to the wedding. If an invitee can't attend the wedding, then they are obliged to give a gift anyway. Feeling a sense of apprehension, many guests go so far as to bring a blank check with them to the wedding, which they later fill in with an amount they feel is commensurate with the type of service they are provided. This way they feel safe knowing that they won't spend too much on a wedding gift. Due to the influence of Kali Yuga, this type of behavior is all too common and it has shifted the entire focus of a wedding from a mood of celebration, to a mood of miserliness. A wedding should be a joyous occasion, a time to share feelings of love and happiness with friends and family. Instead, people have become preoccupied with taking head counts, filling up seats, and tallying the gifts that come in.

From the example of Kings Janaka and Dashratha, we can learn the proper way to celebrate a wedding. A marriage is a joyous occasion, and it should be celebrated as such. In modern society, when a new child is a born, the father typically hands out cigars to friends and family as a way to celebrate. The Vedic example is very similar, except it is done on a larger scale and for every celebratory occasion. The marriage of Sita and Rama involved giving on a grand scale. Brahmanas were given charity and fed sumptuously. Entire villages were invited to the wedding by Janaka with nothing expected in return. Sita was Janaka's pride and joy, so he wanted everyone to share in this most wonderful of occasions. He was getting God Himself as a son-in-law, so of course he would go to great lengths to celebrate their nuptials.

The Vedas represent perfect knowledge, originally passed down from God Himself. They give us the proper guidance we need to manage our daily affairs. Being a good host means following the proper standards of religion set forth in the Vedas. By liberally distributing gifts to the brahmanas, Dashratha secured their blessings upon his sons. We should follow his example by aiming to please the devotees of Krishna.

Devotees are very dear to the Lord, so by pleasing them, we can make our lives perfect.

News We Can Use

"...In our childhood, we saw every village, every town, the transcendental knowledge. Any common man could speak about Ramayana, Mahabharata, Lord Krishna. And system was—still there are, but practically closed now—that in the evening, in the village, everyone should assemble in a place to hear messages from Mahabharata, Ramayana..." (Shrila Prabhupada, Lecture, 720531SB.LA)

"The latest on Michael Jackson...What were the celebs wearing for the big red carpet premiere...Are Brad and Angelina still together?" These stories are all part of the news cycle these days. We are all well acquainted with what is shown to us on the nightly television newscasts and twenty-four hour cable networks. It seems that the stories repeat themselves over and over again. The news media becomes obsessed with celebrity figures and their private lives, and we in turn are kept in the loop. We like to watch the news since it makes us feel like we're keeping up with the times.

The latest news is what's talked about at the water cooler at work. "Did you hear about so and so? Oh boy, I can't believe so and so said that?" These are the typical conversations that take place related to the latest happenings. In the long run, the day to day goings on of celebrities is pretty much useless information. They don't impact our lives in any significant way. If we rewind to one, five, or even ten years ago, we'll see that the news stories were very similar. Some celebrity was getting divorced, another couple started dating, or an athlete was arrested for some nefarious activity. What was labeled as "breaking news" in the past, turned out not to be very important to us. We easily could have survived without hearing about it.

During the ancient Vedic times in India, the source of news and entertainment was the recitation of the Puranas. *Purana* is a Sanskrit word that means "of ancient times", and the Puranas are so named because they are ancient stories relating to God and His associates. The stories deal with the biological ancestry of man, great wars, backbiting, heroism, good, evil, birth, death, etc. Since the stories detail extraordinary events and feats of strength not seen in today's world, many mistakenly believe the Puranas to be mythology, but they are actual historical incidents that took place on this planet and other planets in the universe during this creation and previous ones as well. The Puranas even deal with events that have yet to take place.

Vyasadeva is considered the author of the Puranas in their written form, but prior to that, they were passed down through an oral tradition. Instead of watching television or reading newspapers, the nighttime entertainment consisted of listening to brahmanas, or priests, give recitations of stories relating to Lord Krishna and His various incarnations. People used to gather round and listen very attentively, similar to way people today enjoy hearing campfire stories. These stories were heard so often, that most in society were well versed in their details.

When reading these Puranas today, one will find that references are made to previous incidents, such as wars between the demigods and the demons. Comparisons are often made to great heroes and warriors of the past. "I will defeat you just as the wielder of the thunderbolt defeated Vritrasura." This statement is a reference to the incident where Lord Indra, the chief of the demigods, took on and defeated the demon Vritrasura. This battle is documented in detail in the Bhagavata Purana, but references to it are found in many other books, such as the Valmiki Ramayana. Another comparison that is often made is to that of the fire that takes place when the world ends. The Vedas tell us that this world is constantly going through cycles of creation and destruction. Destruction results from a great fire, caused by Lord Shiva, that envelops the entire earth. When reading the Puranas one will find many references to this with statements such as "When he released his weapon, the impact was so strong that it appeared as if the fire of dissolution had come upon them." These references aren't usually explained in detail because it is inferred that the reader knows all the details. That shows just how well versed the citizens were in the tenets of the Vedas. The citizens were so well educated on matters of religion, that those reciting the stories didn't want to waste time rehashing things that the audience already knew.

Unlike the news, the Puranas contain real information that has everlasting relevance. The Vishnu, Brahmavaivarta, and Bhagavata Puranas, along with the Mahabharata and Ramayana, contain details of the life and pastimes of Lord Krishna and His primary incarnations. There is no higher, more important literature in the world than that which describes God and devotion to Him. These books describe the constitutional position of the soul, why it is put into the material world, and how it can get out and return to the spiritual world.

Of all the Puranas, the Bhagavata Purana, or Shrimad Bhagavatam, is considered the highest. Just as the material world is governed by three qualities or modes, so the eighteen major Puranas are divided by these same qualities. There are six Puranas for each the three *gunas*: goodness, passion, and ignorance. The Shrimad Bhagavatam is one of the *sattvic* Puranas, being in the mode of goodness. Other Puranas delve into many material subjects, such as sacrifices and penances prescribed for material advancement. For this reason, the Mahabharata is generally considered suitable for women and shudras, or those who are less intelligent. The Shrimad Bhagavatam doesn't spend much time discussing the four rewards of material life: *dharma* (religiosity), *artha* (economic development), *kama* (sense gratification), and *moksha* (liberation). Bhakti yoga, or devotional service to Krishna is completely spiritual and above any material activity and is the main focus of the Bhagavatam.

The Bhagavatam deals primarily with Lord Krishna and devotion to Him. It describes in detail the Lord's birth in Mathura and childhood pastimes in Vrindavana. A.C. Bhaktivedanta Swami Prabhupada has translated this voluminous work into English and provided commentary as well. We should take advantage of this wonderful opportunity by reading this book and acquainting ourselves with true Vedic wisdom. We watch the news to increase our knowledge, but one who becomes familiar with the teachings of the Puranas actually becomes the most learned scholar of all.

Politically Incorrect

"Oh best of men, what you have said is not becoming of a mighty prince versed in military arts and is really very opprobrious and infamous. What more, it is not proper even to hear them." (Sita Devi speaking to Lord Rama, Valmiki Ramayana, Ayodhya Kand, Sec 27)

The concept of political correctness has steadily gained in popularity over the years and has now been subscribed to by most in society. Wikipedia defines political correctness as being

"...a term applied to language, ideas, policies, or behavior seen as seeking to minimize offense to gender, racial, cultural, disabled, aged or other identity groups."

It is a concept that germinated from a group of people known as the "offended." This group, which constantly takes offense to statements made about them or others, gave us the idea of "political incorrectness", which is any statement deemed to be purposefully harmful to another group.

Any person can be part of the "offended." Anytime anyone says something that impacts someone else in a negative way, the affected party can claim to be offended. This material world is full of dualities. Hot and cold, good and bad, likes and dislikes are concepts that everyone is familiar with. What may be viewed as beneficial by one person, may be deemed as harmful to another. Certain people like to eat vegetables, while others abhor them. So as soon as we make any statement, as harmless as they may seem to us, there are bound to be people who take umbrage. This phenomenon was never better displayed then during the 1995-96 presidential election season in America. In 1995, General Colin Powell, a well respected military man who had previously served as Chairman of the Joint Chiefs of Staff was contemplating running for the office of President of the United States in the following year's election. General Powell enjoyed tremendously high approval ratings amongst the populace and it was for this reason that he thought about running. However, one fact was overlooked by many. General Powell had yet to take a stance on any major issues. No one knew what he stood for. By staying away from controversial issues, General Powell ensured that the majority of people would like him, for as soon as he declared his stance on abortion or gun control, he was sure to alienate at least half the voting public, which would dramatically affect his approval ratings. He eventually decided against running.

When one makes an opinionated statement, there are bound to be those who disagree not based on the actual merits of the statement, but more on how the opinions make them feel. The person making the statements is then put on defensive and attacked not for the substance of their statements, but for their motives behind making them. "I can't believe that you said that. You're a racist, sexist, bigot, homophobe, etc." is the usual retort of the offended. Common terms such as "African-American", "Hispanic-American", and "undocumented worker" are all products of the political correctness movement. These various groups took umbrage with the words used to describe them, so people subsequently started using terms deemed less offensive. In actuality, almost everyone is suffering from the skin disease brought on by contact with the material world. We can use less offensive terms to describe physical characteristics, but these identifications are still flawed since they don't reference the fact that we are all constitutionally equal.

The motivation behind the political correctness movement is to stifle free speech. Labeling something as "politically incorrect" attaches a stigma to it, and people are less likely to utter such statements. One can read a newspaper or watch cable television to see examples of political incorrectness. A famous celebrity need only utter one statement deemed as offensive, and the media will subsequently run with the story. People naturally will have a negative reaction to such statements, not realizing that everyone one of us is flawed and living on the bodily platform.

Being in the material world means falsely identifying with our bodies and not realizing that we are all constitutionally spirit souls. As spirit souls, we are all equal, yet forgetting that fact, we make generalizations about groups of people based on their physical attributes. In actuality one shouldn't be offended simply by words uttered by others. If we understand the Vedic truth of *aham brahmasmi* (" I am spirit soul"), then we can easily brush aside any statements pertaining to our gross material body.

When Lord Krishna incarnated as Lord Rama many thousands of years ago in Ayodhya, He was ordered to live in the forest for fourteen years by His father, King Dashratha. This all occurred on the very day He was to be installed as the new king. Just prior to leaving town, the Lord went back to His palace and told His wife Sita the news. She was very distraught, and to make matters worse, the Lord instructed her not to accompany Him. He gave her a very erudite sounding speech, stating that her duties were now to serve the new king, Lord Rama's younger brother Bharata. The Lord wanted to protect her from the difficulties of forest life, so He begged her to stay in Ayodhya and await His return fourteen years later.

When Sita Devi heard this, she was very angered. She was Lakshmi herself, the goddess of fortune who is always serving Krishna in the spiritual world. Lakshmi incarnated as Sita Devi as a means of accompanying the Lord in the execution of His pastimes. Sita was greatly offended at the mere thought of being separated from Rama. She immediately chastised Him for even suggesting such a thing. This represents the attitude of a true devotee of the Lord. Devotees can never live without Krishna. Any thought of separation from the Lord is immediately rejected by them.

Such ideas of separation and forgetfulness of our relationship with God represent real political incorrectness. Today there is much talk about God being dead or God not existing. Krishna is accepted as a mere mortal or a manifestation of the impersonal Brahman by many so-called yogis and Vedantists. This sort of speech is what actually needs to be stopped, not mundane statements made about someone's bodily characteristics. Instead of identifying ourselves as American, Indian, black, or white, we should reacquaint ourselves with our true identity, that of servants to Lord Krishna. We should take offense at any blasphemous remarks directed at the Lord and His devotees, the Vaishnavas.

We should learn from Sita Devi's example, and never put up with such talk and refute it every opportunity we get. Lord Rama, being God Himself, is incapable of making offensive remarks but He purposefully made these statements to His wife because He knew they would anger her. He wanted people to learn from her reaction. He knew just how devoted she was to Him, but He wanted everyone else, including future generations, to also witness her display of devotion. "My Lord, you are the only truth. Life without you is a life not worth living. So please do not suggest such a thing." These were the thoughts of Sita and for this she is the perfect woman and devotee.

The Humble Genius

"The grammatical word jugglers cannot bewilder a devotee who engages in chanting the Hare Krishna maha-mantra. Simply addressing the energy of the Supreme Lord as Hare and the Lord Himself as Krishna very soon situates the Lord within the heart of the devotee. By thus addressing Radha and Krishna, one directly engages in His Lordship's service." (Shrila Prabhupada, Chaitanya Charitamrita Adi-lila 7.73 Purport)

The formulaic cable television shows now regularly feature debates between so-called experts in various fields. With the debates usually dealing with issues of politics and public policy, these guests attempt to make clever arguments in favor of their position, trying to sound very erudite in the process. Most of these experts are in fact lawyers by trade, chosen to be on television more for their speaking ability than their actual knowledge of the field they are discussing.

We have all been to parties and other social gatherings where we have encountered the resident "expert". This person has an opinion about everything and can't stop talking. They are thoroughly convinced of their ideas but they are more or less blowing hot air. When we hear someone who isn't an expert discussing issues that we know a lot about, we get insulted very easily. "Who does this person think he is? He is speaking nonsense. He has no idea what such and such really involves." Whether it involves sports, news, or issues relating to our occupation, we all have intimate knowledge of the things that we are passionate about.

According to Vedic philosophy, true knowledge involves the theoretical and the practical, referred to as *jnana* and *vijnana* in Sanskrit. Theoretical knowledge forms the foundation, but it is through practical experience that we truly begin to understand something. The same way that many people pretend to be experts in various subjects, many people pretend to be experts in matters of religion. They have all these dreamed up ideas, but they don't practice any sort of service to God. They develop their own ideas of God and what happens to us after we die. This sort of mental speculation will always lead us down the wrong path since our material minds aren't capable of understanding God on our own. Simply being able to speak well doesn't make one an expert either. The Mayavadis are very expert at using word jugglery to argue their position that God is impersonal and that we are all God. They quote from the Vedanta-sutras and use high class words in their arguments, but their knowledge is nevertheless useless since they fail to recognize Krishna as the Supreme Personality of Godhead.

To truly understand God, we have to take instruction from a real expert in the field, a bona fide spiritual master. A spiritual master, or guru, is one whose only passion is Krishna and who devotes his whole life to Him. He has learned theoretical knowledge through studying the Vedas and by following the instructions from his own spiritual master, and he has acquired practical knowledge through practicing the principles of devotional service. In the Bhagavad-gita, Lord Krishna, God Himself, instructs His dear friend Arjuna to seek out a spiritual master.

"Just try to learn the truth by approaching a spiritual master. Inquire from him submissively and render service unto him. The self-realized soul can impart knowledge unto you because he has seen the truth." (Lord Krishna, BG 4.34)

The key is to enquire submissively. If we are hostile towards our spiritual master, then we will never learn anything. We encounter these situations often when engaging in friendly talks with others. If we state a strongly held belief or opinion, many people question us or take the opposite position simply as a way of starting an argument. This is called playing devil's advocate, which Wikipedia defines as:

"In common parlance, a devil's advocate is someone who takes a position he or she disagrees with for the sake of argument. This process can be used to test the quality of the original argument and identify weaknesses in its structure."

Taking this sort of approach with a spiritual master isn't a good idea. A devotee of Krishna is very kind by nature and readily willing to impart instruction to those who sincerely seek it. However, if a guru notes a tone of hostility in a person, they will not be likely to continue instructing them. This doesn't mean that we shouldn't pose questions to our guru, but these questions shouldn't be in a challenging spirit. Questions should be relevant to the topics being discussed and they should be asked with the intention of furthering one's knowledge of the Vedas. The Puranas, Mahabharata, and Ramayana all have great examples of how one should conduct themselves in front of a spiritual master. In the Bhagavata Purana, known as the Shrimad Bhagavatam, Maharaja Parikshit, a great king descending from the Pandava family, takes instruction from Shukadeva Goswami. In a very submissive manner, asking questions very nicely, Parikshit shows us that if we respect our spiritual master, then he will reward us with the highest knowledge. The Bhagavatam details the life and pastimes of Lord Krishna when He descended to earth. It was due to Parikshit's inquisitiveness and service to Shukadeva Goswami that we are able to benefit from such stories today.

In the Ramacharitamanasa, an incident is described where Lord Rama, an incarnation of Lord Krishna, visits the hermitage of Maharishi Valmiki in the forest. Along with His wife Sita and younger brother Lakshmana, the Lord was wandering through the forest serving an exile period ordered by His father. Now Rama was God Himself, yet when He saw Valmiki, the Lord immediately prostrated Himself before the great sage and asked him very nicely where He and His family could go and set up a cottage. Valmiki was very pleased with Rama, for he knew

His divinity. Instead of telling them where to set up camp, Valmiki gave a beautiful description on the qualities of a devotee, stating that Sita, Rama, and Lakshmana should always live in the hearts of such people. If the the Lord Himself submits to a spiritual master, then we should also follow suit.

Knowledge of Krishna and the Vedas has been passed down from time immemorial through the guru-disciple relationship. In the Bhagavad-gita, Lord Krishna explains that He first imparted spiritual knowledge to the sun god at the beginning of creation, and that same knowledge was then passed down through the chain of disciplic succession, or the *parampara* system. Periodically this chain gets broken and Krishna Himself comes to reinstitute it.

Lord Krishna is the original guru, but He Himself has told us to take instruction from a spiritual master, so we should heed His advice. A.C. Bhaktivedanta Swami Prabhupada is the spiritual master for this age. Though we cannot personally approach him, he left behind a wealth of knowledge in his books and recorded lectures. One can find answers to all of life's questions by steadily reading and rereading these wonderful books. Following the instructions of the spiritual master, we can become the greatest experts in the most important science, the science of devotional service.

In Sickness and In Health

"Oh dear husband…father, mother, son, brother, daughter-in-law, all of them abide by the consequences of their own actions, it is the wife alone, Oh best of men, that shares the fate of her husband; it is therefore that ever along with you I have been ordered to live in the forest." (Sita Devi speaking to Lord Rama, Valmiki Ramayana, Ayodhya Kand, Section 27)

In Western society weddings are typically held in churches with a priest presiding over the ceremony. The bride and groom make their way to the altar, and then recite vows usually prepared beforehand. Recitation of these vows in the presence of a priest makes the wedding official. As part of the standard vows recited at most weddings, the bride and groom both promise to love each other in "sickness and in health". The phrase that then follows is "til death do us part." Even though such vows are made, we see that many marriages still end in divorce. So what goes wrong?

Starting with the women's suffrage movement in 1920s, women have gradually been given more and more independence in society. Unlike the past, women play a prominent role in the work place and are given the same educational opportunities as men. Now free to pursue their own careers, women's roles in marriages have drastically changed. In the past, they played the traditional role of a housewife, someone who would take care of the kids and manage the household affairs while the husband would go out and earn a living. In the modern age, both the man and the woman typically work in order to support the family. During the day, children are often dropped off in daycare centers or left under the care of babysitters or family members. The cost of living has dramatically increased, so in many instances two incomes are required to maintain a family.

The motives behind wanting independence and a career are very noble. There is nothing wrong with it in general. However, when we focus on our careers, other things in our life naturally will receive less attention. This holds true for both men and women. What can happen over time is that the husband and wife will gradually drift apart. Putting their personal interests ahead of their partner's, the relationship suffers. Jealousy, anger, and resentment subsequently follow, all of which inevitably lead to divorce. The original marriage vows become dissolved in an instant through the help of the legal system. The marriage in essence doesn't amount to anything more than a piece of paper.

Divorce is a tragic thing and it leaves us searching for answers as to what could have been done to prevent it. Authors of self-help books and relationship advice doctors make millions trying to solve this very problem. Television programs hosted by Oprah Winfrey and Dr. Phil often deal with the subject of husband-wife relations, and these shows get very high ratings. The general consensus seems to be that relationships need more communication. The modern theory is that the husband and wife should both have equality in the relationship and that there needs to be compromise. We see this message being preached everywhere, but it doesn't seem to be providing any results.

So what can be done to actually solve the problem? The answer can be found in the Vedas, the ancient teachings of India dating back to the beginning of time. According to Vedic doctrine, each one of us is responsible for our actions. We suffer both the good and bad consequences of our actions through the laws of karma. This belief is universal and is found in all religions. The Vedas make an exception however, in the case of married women. For a married women, her only dharma, or religious duty, is to serve her husband. Now many people often misinterpret this to mean that the wife should be the slave of the husband. That is not the case. On the contrary, the Vedas teach us that both the husband and wife have equality, but not how we think of it. Their equality lies in their fate. They are both spirit souls, with the wife's spiritual fate being bound to her husband's. It is for this reason that a girl should be married off to a man who is very pious. If a wife faithfully serves a pious husband, then she earns all the religious merits of her husband. If her husband is very sinful, then the wife will also suffer the consequences of his actions. It is for this reason that the Vedas instruct the wife to faithfully serve the husband and ensure that he remains on the proper path of virtue.

Lord Rama, an incarnation of Krishna, appeared in Ayodhya many thousands of years ago. As the eldest son of the king, Maharaja Dashratha, Rama was the heir apparent to the throne. On the day He was to be coronated, Dashrata instead banished the Lord to the forest for fourteen years. This order was enacted due to a promise the king had made to one of his wives, Kaikeyi. After hearing of the new plans, Lord Rama went back to His palace to tell His wife Sita the bad news. In telling her, the Lord instructed Sita to remain in Ayodhya and faithfully serve the king and other family members until His return. Sita Devi vehemently disagreed with the Lord's decision not to take her, and gave a stirring speech in hopes of persuading Rama to allow her to accompany Him. Sita was the incarnation of Lakshmi, who is the eternal consort of Narayana, or God. Sita never wants to be separated from Rama and it for this reason that she refused to remain in the kingdom.

From her statements, we can see that she was the perfect woman. Her husband was the king's favorite son and had all the riches in the world. Now that He was banished to the forest, where He would live a life akin to a homeless person, Sita still didn't think any less of Him. "What happens to You, happens to me. Don't think of me as being a separate person from You. We are one." is what she thought. She stood by Her man, in sickness and in health. This is the example of a perfect wife.

Sita Devi spoke eloquently about the duties of a wife, but in actuality she was teaching us how to be perfect devotees. Sita's decision to go to the forest was completely up to her. She could have easily remained in the kingdom and lived very comfortably. Instead, she voluntarily chose to subject herself to the austere conditions of forest life. She did this so that she could remain with Lord Rama, who was God Himself. This is the path laid out for all of us. The Vedas refer to the voluntary acceptance of austerities as *tapasya*. *Tapasya* means performing austerities for a spiritual benefit and for no other reason. Sita performed *tapasya* so that God would be pleased with her. We should follow her example and perform our own tapasya by abstaining from the four pillars of sinful life, namely meat eating, gambling, intoxication, and illicit sex life. Just like Sita, if we give up material pleasures as a sacrifice to the Lord and always chant his names "**Hare Krishna Hare Krishna, Krishna Krishna, Hare Hare, Hare Rama Hare Rama, Rama Rama, Hare Hare**", then we too will get to follow Him wherever He goes.

Everlasting Fame

"Oh Hanuman! Your magnificent glory is acclaimed far and wide all through the four ages and your fame is radiantly noted all over the cosmos." (Hanuman Chalisa of Tulsidas)

Social networking websites have greatly increased in popularity. It seems that everyone has a MySpace, Twitter, or Facebook page. These sites make it very easy to connect with other people quickly and to share information and thoughts.

Of all these sites, Facebook has stood out as the premier social networking engine. Facebook allows you to upload pictures of yourself, describe your hobbies and interests, and make friends with a large network of people. Instead of having to contact all of your friends individually, you can just update your Facebook profile and broadcast updates about yourself to all of your friends. Your friends in turn can post responses to you or to your "wall", creating a message board like atmosphere.

The popularity of Facebook lies in its ability to make anyone famous. We all want to be noticed and to matter. When something good happens to us, we immediately can't wait to tell our friends. When we are sad, we take comfort in the soothing words and advice from our well-wishers. Similar to how the news media follows every move of celebrities, Facebook allows others to follow our every move. In this way, we can achieve fame and notoriety without ever having to leave our homes.

This fame and notoriety is no doubt very pleasing to us, but it has a very short duration. We are all destined to give up our current bodies at the time of death, and when we do, we give up our fame as well. From studying Vedic literature, we can see that the best way to have everlasting fame is to become a devotee of Krishna, or God. When we sincerely love God and devote ourselves to Him only, then He will automatically give us all the fame that we crave. There are many examples of this principle holding true, with four in particular that stand out.

When God advented as Lord Rama many thousands of years ago in Ayodhya, as part of His pastimes, He suffered through many trials and tribulations. One ordeal He endured was the kidnapping of His wife Sita by the demon Ravana. Though a prince and son of a great king, Lord Rama was serving His exile period in the forest at the time, so He had no army with which to attack Ravana and reclaim Sita. Instead, He enlisted the help of Vanaras, or human-like monkeys, which were dwelling in the forest. The foremost of the Vanaras was Lord Hanuman. Hanuman was a great devotee of Lord Rama and he played an integral part in helping the Lord defeat Ravana and rescue Sita. In reward for his devotion, Lord Rama blessed Hanuman and granted him the boon of remaining on earth for as long as the Lord's story was still told and His glories still chanted. Hanuman had no desire for this fame, but the Lord granted it to him anyway. Hanuman is still worshiped to this day and his name is synonymous with love and devotion for Lord Rama.

When Lord Krishna personally came to earth some five thousand years ago, there was a great war that took place on the battlefield of Kurukshetra between the Pandava and Kaurava families. Lord Krishna was very fond of His cousin Arjuna, the leading warrior for the Pandavas, so He acted as Arjuna's charioteer and guide. The great grandfather of both families, Bhishma, was one of the leading fighters on the Kaurava side. Bhishma was eventually defeated by Arjuna in battle. While he was lying on the ground, his body pierced throughout with arrows, Lord Krishna instructed Yudhishthira, the eldest of the five Pandava brothers, to go to Bhishma and receive spiritual instruction from him. Bhishma was a great devotee of the Lord, and had his mind concentrated on Krishna while he was lying on the battlefield about to die. The Lord knew this and thus wanted

Yudhishthira to question such a great devotee. The Lord could have taught Yudhishthira Himself, but He preferred to have Bhishma do it. God is always glad to give fame to His devotees. As much as His devotees like to please Him, the Lord prefers to give His devotees all the fame and glory.

Maharishi Valmiki, the great sage and author of the Ramayana, incarnated some four hundred years ago in India as Goswami Tulsidas. Tulsidas was a great devotee of Lord Rama from birth, and he dedicated his whole life to worshiping and writing about the Lord. His book, the Ramacharitamanasa, is revered to this very day. Tulsidas had no desire for fame or fortune. He wrote only for himself so that he could put his love for Lord Rama into words. The Ramacharitamanasa is the story of Lord Rama written as beautiful poetry in the mood of pure devotion. From reading his books, one will find that Tulsidas was one of the most humble and kind people to ever have lived. Because of his pure devotion, the Lord guaranteed him everlasting fame. His Ramacharitamanasa is today a staple in the homes of all Hindus in India. It is publicly recited during the auspicious times of the year relating to Lord Rama. Tulsidas's poem praising Lord Hanuman, known as the Hanuman Chalisa, is equally as popular and is memorized and recited daily by millions of Hindus as well. All glories to Tulsidas.

His Divine Grace A.C. Bhaktivedanta Swami Prabhupada, the founder of the International Society for Krishna Consciousness, made the name Krishna known throughout the world. Instructed by his spiritual master to preach the teachings of the Vedas in English to the western world, Shrila Prabhupada came to America on a steamship from India in 1965. In the twelve years that followed, he authored almost one hundred books and started a worldwide movement dedicated to serving Lord Krishna that continues to this very day. Though the swami left this material world more than thirty years ago, he continues to teach through his books and recorded lectures. He is worshiped as the spiritual master in hundreds of temples throughout the world and in the homes of devotees. He also had no desire for fame and fortune. His only desire was to make the world love Krishna even more than he himself did. Krishna recognized this devotion and thus made him one of the most famous saints to ever have lived.

These are just some of the examples of famous devotees. In the Bhagavad-gita, Lord Krishna tells Arjuna to "declare it to the world that My devotee shall never perish." So let all devotees of the world unite and spread the glories of Lord Krishna on Facebook and every other social networking site. This will be most beneficial to us, for it will give us everlasting fame. If we love Krishna and are truly devoted to Him, then He will surely make all our wishes come true.

Rising To The Challenge

"If a devotee is intelligent enough, he will make progress on the path of self-realization. If one is sincere and devoted to the activities of devotional service, the Lord gives him a chance to make progress and ultimately attain to Him." (Shrila Prabhupada, Bhagavad-gita 10.10 Purport)

Many of us are born with an innate challenging spirit, arising from the mode of passion. We love to take on challenges and see if we can conquer them. Whether it is running a marathon, skiing down a mountain, competing in an office football pool, or even building something with our hands, we love taking on challenges and seeing if we can come out successful.

We are all part and parcel of the Supreme Personality of Godhead, Lord Krishna, so all of our qualities originate from Him. The material world is a reflection of the spiritual world. Everything that exists here, exists in the spiritual world but in purified form. For example, sex life in the material world is a perverted reflection of the real love that is exchanged on the spiritual planets. The loving affairs of Radha and Krishna aren't anything like the ordinary love affairs of men and women on this earth. It is completely pure in nature, representing the highest form of bliss. Love in the material world, as we think it to be, is actually a form of lust.

"...Just like Radha-Krishna love, *Kishora-kishori*, young Krishna, young Radharani. This love is pervertedly reflected in this material world which is in the name of love, but it is lust; therefore it is called perverted reflection. Lust because the, a young boy, a young girl mix together, they love together, but a slight disagreement, they separate. Why? Because that is not love. That is lust. The lust is going on in the name of love. But the reflection is from there. Therefore it is called maya." (Shrila Prabhupada, Lecture, 690425LE.BOS)

Krishna sometimes feels in the mood to challenge enemies and fight, so He creates situations in this world where that desire can be facilitated. The challenging spirit that exists inside of us is also a skewed reflection of the spirit that exists in the spiritual world. In the material world, we all have a desire to boost our ego and self-esteem. The material world is made up of five gross elements (earth, water, fire, air, and ether) and three subtle elements (mind, intelligence, and false ego). It is referred to as false ego, because it is the nature of man to falsely think himself to be the proprietor of things. Real ego comes when realize that God is responsible for everything and that our duty is to become His servant.

We all like to think of ourselves as special and extraordinary. Taking on new challenges is our way of supporting our ego and increasing our self-respect. Exercising this challenging spirit on tasks in the material world may be very nice, but in the end it really has no lasting effects. Once we conquer a challenge, we immediately need another one to maintain our ego. The great basketball player Michael Jordan won three consecutive NBA titles and multiple Most Valuable Player awards halfway through his career. He was already considered the greatest basketball player ever, so he felt that he needed a new challenge. Retiring from basketball, he took up baseball, playing in the minor leagues for the Chicago White Sox franchise. Unable to succeed in that venture, he eventually returned to basketball where he would go on to win three more NBA titles. This shows that even when we achieve all of our goals, we are still left wanting more, for our desires never become truly satisfied. The mind is constantly working. Being in the material world means we are always hankering after something we want or lamenting over something that we don't have.

The best use of this challenging spirit is to use it in our service to God. Serving Krishna involves following many rules and regulations in the beginning, specifically that of following the four regulative principles and chanting the Hare Krishna mantra. The four regulative principles require abstention from meat eating, gambling, intoxication, and illicit sex. For most people, these restrictions seem very hard to follow. Those growing up in America are quite accustomed to eating meat. The beef industry runs television commercials using the slogan "Beef. It's what's for dinner." The quintessential American meal consists of meat and potatoes. This being the case, it is very difficult for people to suddenly give up meat eating. One doesn't have to renounce everything in the material world in order to make spiritual advancement. Instead we can spiritualize material things by using them to further develop our Krishna consciousness. We can start by using our challenging spirit to help us refrain from prohibited activities. We can dare ourselves not to eat meat for a day, or for a week. Many of us have had bad experiences from intoxication which make us we swear that we'll never drink again. Quitting anything cold turkey is very difficult to do. Instead of completely swearing off of it, maybe we can try avoiding intoxication for a few days or weeks. We can create intoxication-free streaks and reward ourselves after we pass certain milestones. Once we pass such challenges, we can create new goals for ourselves. In this way, we make real advancement and change our habits at the same time. Once we get in the habit of living a clean lifestyle, those habits will be very hard to break. These same techniques can be used to strengthen our chanting regimen. Slowly but surely, if we develop a nice routine, we can easily give up sinful activity and instead focus our time on devotional service.

The highest goal in life is for one to always be thinking of Krishna and have his consciousness completely dovetailed with the spiritual consciousness. This is a very difficult task and many are not successful even after many many births. Lord Krishna Himself declared in the Bhagavad-gita that one who is unsuccessful in transcendental realization in this life, picks up where he left off in his next life. In this way, our efforts in serving Krishna never go to waste. If we challenge ourselves and are sincere in our devotion, then our success is guaranteed.

Our Only Support System

"Neither the father, mother, son, friends, nor her own self is the stay of a woman in this nor in the afterlife; it is the husband alone that is her only support." (Sita Devi speaking to Lord Rama, Valmiki Ramayana, Ayodhya Kand, Sec 27)

In Vedic culture, it is very important for a father to marry off his daughter when she reaches the appropriate age. This statement by Sita Devi explains the reason behind this. More important than anything else, a woman's path to spiritual salvation depends on a good husband.

Over the past one hundred years, throughout the world, society at large has changed. Through democracy and liberation movements in America and abroad, men and women have been given independence, feeling more liberated than ever before. Not only changes in government, but advancements in technology have significantly changed our way of life. In days past, most people were engaged in agriculture, and even cow protection in India. Today's employment landscape is quite different.

"Farm employment peaked between 1840 and 1870. In 1900, 40 percent of American workers were employed in farming; today, it's less than two percent. Technological advances made that possible." (Walter Williams, Foreign Trade Angst)

Going into the workplace and drawing a salary gives people a feeling of self-worth and independence. However, is it really independence? Instead of staying at home and living off the food produced on one's own land, we now are dependent on our bosses, the business managers. Businessmen are by definition interested in one thing, that of earning a profit. We like to think that people start a business so that they can provide good paying jobs to others, but that is a secondary concern. A person doesn't undertake all the risks involved in starting up a business unless they are seeking a substantial return on their investment. Our family, on the other hand, has only our interests at heart. With the wife taking care of the house and the children, and the husband in charge of economic development, both parties are pleased, which leads to happy family life. This sort of family has been replaced with one where husband and wife constantly argue and quarrel since they have their own career interests.

According to Vedic philosophy, a woman is never to be given independence. In her youth, she is protected by her father. As an adult, the husband provides for the wife, and in old age, the eldest son is charge of her protection. Many people misconstrue this to mean that women are treated as servants. In actuality, this system was passed down by God for our benefit. The purpose of human life is to know and understand God. The animal species lack the intelligence to even enquire about God. They spend all their time involved in activities of eating, sleeping, mating, and defending. Since they are completely unaware of dharma, they are incapable of committing sin. The first instruction of the Vedanta-sutras is *athatho brahma-jijnasa* meaning "now is the time to enquire about Brahman". Brahman is God, the Supreme Absolute Truth. If we simply engross ourselves in animalistic activities, then we aren't making proper use of this human form of life.

Working is a necessary evil since the body requires maintenance in order to stay fit in its service to God. The idea is that we should only work to provide the bare necessities of life. It is not that men are supposed to have fun advancing in a career while the wife is left to suffer at home. A marriage is a partnership, with both parties working together for a common interest. A husband and wife share in their religious merits. If a husband is pious and devoted to Krishna, then the wife will follow Him back to Godhead after this life. A father, mother, or even son can definitely prove beneficial to a woman, but they alone are not capable of delivering her to the spiritual world. However, if a woman has a husband who is a pure devotee of Krishna, even if she isn't perfectly pious herself, then she will share in the spiritual rewards bestowed on the husband. Thus it is in the interest of parents to find the most suitable husbands for their daughters.

Sita Devi was the incarnation of Goddess Lakshmi, the husband of Narayana, who is God Himself. It is because of this that one of Krishna's names is Madhava, meaning the husband of the goddess of fortune. When Lord Rama was exiled to the forest, he tried very hard to dissuade His wife Sita from following Him. She adamantly disagreed with Him and the above quote was part of her plea to Him. Having been instructed on Vedic tenets during her childhood by her father and mother, Sita had a perfect understanding of the rules of propriety. Lord Rama set forth very logical arguments in favor of His position that she remain in the kingdom, but Sita's counter-arguments were even stronger. Devotees aren't afraid to argue with the Lord if it means that He will be happier in the end. She knew that the Lord would be pleased by having her accompany Him, so for this reason she wasn't hesitant in arguing with her husband.

Though she was talking generally about husband and wives, the actual lesson she was giving us is that women should accept Krishna, or God as their husband. Krishna is capable of supporting thousands and thousands of wives, as He did during His time on earth some five thousand years ago, so it is in the best interest of all women to accept Him as their husband, at least in their minds. If we all depend on Krishna, then He will support us in any and all situations in this life and the next.

Good Fortune

"...Never consider yourself to be the cause of the results of your activities..." (Lord Krishna speaking to Arjuna, Bhagavad-gita, 2.47)

We all know certain people who seem to be luckier than others. No matter what the situation, things always seem to work out for them, while for others the opposite situation is true. No matter how much effort they put in or how hard they try, things always go wrong for them.

In the 1980s there was a popular children's television cartoon show by the name of Inspector Gadget. The show focused on the crime fighting escapades of the main character, Inspector Gadget, who was sort of a bumbler. He had all these special gadgets at his disposal to help him fight crime, but he never knew how to operate them properly. Each episode had a similar story line: the villain, Dr. Claw, had some elaborate scheme hatched up and Gadget was deputed to try and stop it. However, he would always be led astray, going completely down the wrong path. Gadget always had his niece Penny there to help him. She would always manage to solve the mystery along with help from her dog Brain, and then give the credit to her father. In this way, Dr. Claw's plans were always thwarted, leaving him to utter his famous phrase at the end of each show, "I'll get you Gadget!"

In the sport of tennis, the most prestigious tournament is Wimbledon. Occurring annually in London, it is the title coveted by all tennis players, for it has a rich tradition associated with it. World number one Roger Federer, who many consider the greatest player of all time, has won Wimbledon six times, while fellow player Andy Roddick has never won it. The two have played against each other in the final round of Wimbledon on three separate occasions, with Federer winning every time. In the 2004 final, it appeared that Roddick had Federer's number. Playing very well and taking the opening set, he had Federer on the ropes. In Wimbledon and the other three Grand Slam tournaments, the first player to win three sets wins the match. Towards the end of the second set, Federer was up 6-5 with Roddick serving to force a tiebreaker. In tennis, players alternative service games in a set until one player wins 6 games leading by 2. If the score reaches 6-6, then they play a twelve point tiebreaker to determine the winner of the set. Roddick was two points away from forcing a tiebreaker when suddenly, one of Federer's shots hit the net chord and dribbled over, giving him a set point. Federer would win the next point to even the match at one set all. Roddick still played tough though, as he was leading in the third set when all of a sudden it started raining. Federer regrouped during the rain delay and rallied to win the third set and eventually the match.

In the 2009 Wimbledon final, the two met again, and this time it really looked like Roddick was going to win. After winning the first set, Roddick went up 6 points to 2 in the second set tiebreaker. The first player to win seven points leading by at least two points wins a tiebreaker. With four set points in hand, it seemed for sure that Roddick would take a commanding lead in the match. However, Federer rallied and pulled off a miracle by coming back and winning the tiebreaker, leveling the match at one set all. Roddick would continue to hang tough, as the two played an epic fifth and deciding set. In most Grand Slam tournaments, players don't play a tiebreaker in the fifth set. This means that play continues until one player has a lead of at least two games. The two duked it out, until Federer finally won 16-14, making it one of the greatest tennis matches ever to be played. Once again Roddick came up short. In tennis, if a player can regularly hold serve, meaning win the games in which they are serving, they have an excellent chance of winning. Roddick not only held serve regularly, but he didn't lose serve for the entire match until the very last game. He played the match of his life, and STILL lost.

Now obviously being successful in tennis or other sports requires more than just luck. However, the lesson we can take away from these examples is that we are not the doer. As much as we may think ourselves to be the cause of actions and results, we are not. Lord Krishna, the Supreme Personality of Godhead, and His energies are responsible for making the world go around. Our karma also plays a role, determining our future fortunes and misfortunes.

"The bewildered spirit soul, under the influence of the three modes of material nature, thinks himself to be the doer of activities, which are in actuality carried out by nature." (Lord Krishna, Bhagavad-gita, 3.27)

This is the central tenet of the Vedas. When Krishna incarnated on earth as the pious prince Lord Rama, He underwent many hardships. Things always seemed to go wrong for the Lord, with His father exiling Him from the kingdom and His wife being kidnapped by the demon Ravana. As bad as things got, the Lord and His younger brother Lakshmana always remained steady. In the Ramayana, the two brothers make many references to the fact that destiny and fate control everything and that we are not the doers. If a higher power is in charge of everything, then we have no reason to overly lament over bad times or to overly rejoice over good fortune.

Now this doesn't mean that we shouldn't act. It'd be very easy to just say, "Well, I don't have any control over anything, so I'm just going to stop all of my activities altogether." The key is to act without attachment to the results of our actions.

"Be steadfast in yoga, O Arjuna. Perform your duty and abandon all attachment to success or failure. Such evenness of mind is called yoga." (Lord Krishna, Bhagavad-gita, 2.48)

The easiest way to do this is to perform everything for the pleasure of the Lord. Acting only to please Him and to make Him happy, we free ourselves from the effects of karma. Happiness and sadness, distress and relief, these are the dualities of material nature that come and go. We should rise above them by directing our actions towards pleasing the Supreme Lord Krishna. If we become attached to Him, then His wife, the goddess of fortune, will see it to that we always have the proper means at our disposal to carry out our service. Often thought of as the giver of wealth, she actually provides good fortune to us so that we may use it properly. Goddess Lakshmi is always serving the Supreme Lord in the spiritual world, so she bestows her blessings on those people who will act in the same way. By sincerely taking to devotional service, we can be assured of always having good luck.

The Inconceivable

"Just like Krishna is lifting the hill, then what is the difficulty for God to lift a hill if He is all-powerful? But as soon as they read it, that Krishna is lifting hill, they will take it as mythology. So when God shows that "I am God," that is mythology, and they imagine God. That is rascaldom. When God comes and shows His godly power, they take it as myth, mythology. And they imagine God according to your definition. Is that sanity?" (Shrila Prabhupada)

Comment: The scriptures shouldn't be interpreted literally but should be looked at more for their inner meaning and symbolism.

Response: The Vedas, Mahabharata, and Puranas are all retellings of historical events that took place on this planet and others. Not only past events are covered, but even events that have yet to occur are discussed in detail in these wonderful books, such as the Bhavishya and Kalki Puranas. Since these books contain direct quotations from conversations between great personalities, demigods, and even God Himself, they must be taken literally. We shouldn't try to imagine the true meaning behind someone's quote, or even think that these events didn't take place.

Conversations are conversations. When we talk with our friends in person, on the phone, or through email, they are exchanges of ideas and comments. Very simply put, what we say is what we say. We may go back and not like some of the things we have said, but it doesn't mean that we didn't say them. In the same way, the Vedic literatures have conversations between God and His associates, and also conversations between spiritual masters and their disciples. These conversations were specifically chronicled in written form for the benefit of current and future generations of man. The science of self-realization described in the original Vedas and the Vedanta-sutras can appear to be very complicated to many, for it has various aphorisms and postulates that neophytes will have trouble understanding. For this reason, the

Puranas, Ramayana, and other great works contain those same teachings but told in the form of stories and conversations.

There are many instances described in the Vedic texts that may seem extraordinary to us. Lord Rama killing 14,000 Rakshasa demons all by Himself, Lord Krishna as a small child lifting a hill with just one finger, Gandhari giving birth to 100 sons...all these seem extraordinary to the common man, for we can't fathom someone doing these things. God is great. This is the belief of people of all faiths. Yet the Vedas go one step further by trying to describe just how great He is. Of course, God's greatness is inconceivable. His is described as *paramam* or Supreme because He possesses six opulences in full and simultaneously. We don't know any single person who is the wealthiest, most beautiful, most famous, the strongest, the most knowledgeable, and the greatest renunciate at the same time. Yet Krishna possesses all of these attributes, and for this reason He is God. Just because we don't know anyone capable of performing these great feats, we shouldn't think that these incidents are merely fabrications of someone's mind. These sages who composed the Vedic literature were all perfect souls. Having surrendered everything for the service of Krishna, they were given the divine vision to see all these things happen and then be able to write about them. The great Maharishi Valmiki described the events of the Ramayana before they even occurred.

If we think that these incidents are just mythology, then we lose our ability to understand God. In actuality, we can never truly understand God for His is beyond our comprehension. However, through faithfully studying the scriptures under the guidance of a bona fide spiritual master, we can start to understand Him to some extent. The Lord and His spiritual master must be approached in a humble manner. We all at some point in our life have prayed to God for something. "Please God give me this, give me that, make sure my family is healthy, etc." The understanding that God is great is something inside of us, part of our core. If we challenge Him, or start thinking that His scriptures are mere mythology, then we are cheating God. We may cheat our friends, coworkers, or enemies and be able to get away with it, but cheating God never pays. He knows and sees all, so if we cheat Him, we are only cheating ourselves. The Bhagavad-gita is probably the most famous Vedic literature, detailing the conversation that took place on the battlefield of Kurukshetra between Lord Krishna and Arjuna some five thousand years ago. There are many high scholars and philosophers who have commented on the Bhagavad-gita, all with the purpose of advancing their own opinions. Many of them have postulated that the events of the Gita actually never happened and that we should study it simply for its symbolism. The ultimate conclusion of the Gita is that people should surrender unto Krishna or God and become His devotee. The flowery language that precedes that is all meaningless unless one comes to the proper conclusion as stated by the Lord Himself. Those who extract any other meaning from the Gita are only cheating God. He has given us such a nice book for us to learn from, so we shouldn't dishonor Him by making false conclusions.

The Vedic literature should be heard from devotees, otherwise we become prone to believing some of these false theories put forward by mental speculators and pseudo-yogis. Shukadevi Goswami, Vyasadeva, Narada Muni, etc. are all great devotees who presented these works in a mood of devotion. The various quotes and teachings found in the Vedas should also be understood in the proper context. One can pull out quotes to buttress their positions, but these statements should be understood with the full context presented at the same time. For example, there are many conversations in the Vedas where women are criticized for having various shortcomings. However, these faults don't exist in people who are great devotees, be they men or women. The material world is full of dualities, so any mundane argument will naturally have a counterargument. There may be different teachings presented due to time and circumstance and the ability of the people at the time to grasp Vedic wisdom, but the end goal is always the same. The purpose of the Vedas is to present everything in relation to Krishna, who is the Supreme Absolute Truth. Since He is completely spiritual, mundane dualities don't exist when discussing topics relating to Him.

It is natural that occasionally certain statements in the Vedas will rub us the wrong away. However, just because we might not agree with them at the time, doesn't mean that the Vedas are at fault. When we were younger, our parents prohibited us from taking part in many activities. These rules and regulations angered us very much and we thought our parents were in the wrong for imposing such restrictions. However, as we got older, we not only realized that our parents were correct, but we started imposing the same rules on our children. In the same way, the Vedas represent perfect knowledge. The rules and regulations prescribed are those coming down from God Himself, so they cannot be faulty. We may disagree with them, but that is our problem, not God's. If Krishna or one of His associates say something, we must accept it as fact.

The great founder-acharya of the International Society for Krishna Consciousness, A.C. Bhaktivedanta Swami Prabhupada, summarized all of the Vedic teachings in his numerous books and recorded lectures. One simply needs to consult his teachings in order to gain a firm grasp on the Vedic tenets. Since he was a pure devotee, his explanations and commentaries are perfect. We may not agree with everything in the beginning, but if we continue reading and stay connected with Prabhupada, then we will become perfect devotees.

The Most Romantic

"If do you repair today to the forest impregnable, I shall go before you, oh Raghava, treading upon the thorns and prickly grass." (Sita Devi speaking to Lord Rama, Valmiki Ramayana, Ayodhya Kand, Sec 27)

We are all familiar with the typical storyline of romance films. A guy meets a girl and they both take a liking to each other, but there is something keeping them from being together. Sometimes the woman isn't sure if the man is right for her and she wants more evidence that he really loves her. Sensing this, the man will go out of his way to be more romantic. Buying flowers, writing love letters, and hatching elaborate schemes are all part of the guy's plan to win the girl over her. He woos her in hopes of sweeping her off her feet and eventually living happily ever after.

These movies typically end happily with the guy and the girl overcoming whatever obstacles were in their way. These stories usually stop here, and we don't get to see what happens to the couple once they enter married life. As evidenced by the high divorce rate in America, real life relationships often dissolve due to disagreements and the loss of affection. The man has already chased after the girl and caught her, so he no longer feels obligated to be romantic and spontaneous. The woman misses this romantic side of her husband, and gradually starts to feel unappreciated. Feeling this way, the woman starts to wonder whether or not her husband still loves her. No one likes to love somebody and not be loved back, so this situation leads to bitterness. Bitterness leads to disagreements, which lead to full blown arguments, which can eventually lead to divorce.

Lord Rama was a special incarnation of Lord Krishna that appeared on this earth many thousands of years ago in the city of Ayodhya. He played the role of a pious prince, completely dedicated to the welfare of His dependents and well-wishers. When God comes to earth, He brings along His closest associates to help Him in the execution of His mission. Lord Rama was married to Sita Devi, the incarnation of Goddess Lakshmi. In the spiritual world, Lakshmi is the eternal consort of Narayana, or God, serving to His every need. More than just a wife, she is a perfect devotee who brings good fortune and wealth to all those who please her. Her intimate association with God brings her the most pleasure, thus Lord Narayana is the most fortunate and the wealthiest. As Sita Devi, Lakshmi mimicked the role she plays in the spiritual world, dedicating her life to the welfare and good fortune of her husband.

As the eldest son of the king of Ayodhya, Maharaja Dashratha, Rama was next in line for the throne. When He reached the appropriate age, all preparations were made by Dashratha for his son's installation. However, on the day set for Rama's installation, the plans were suddenly changed, with Rama's younger brother Bharata chosen to ascend the throne instead. In conjunction with this directive, the Lord was ordered to leave the kingdom and not return for fourteen years. Rama agreed to these two orders from His father, for He had no attachment to the throne nor to the worldly pleasures afforded Him in the kingdom.

After being given the order to spend fourteen years living as a homeless recluse in the forest by His father, Rama went to His beautiful and faithful wife Sita to break the bad news to her. Though having already been married for twelve years, the couple was still in love, and Rama wanted to protect her. He instructed Sita to remain in the kingdom during the exile period and not to worry about Him. He gave her a great dissertation on the duties of a wife and the dangers of forest life. Sita was raised as the most beloved daughter of King Janaka of Mithila, so she was always accustomed to living the life of a princess. Forest life was meant for the very toughest of men, those who had their senses under control, and who had no attachments to worldly comforts. Lord

Rama, being God Himself, was the ultimate renunciate, so living in the forest would be no problem for Him. Yet Sita was a woman, and being of the fairer sex, she held a privileged status in society. We often hear the term "women and children first" when referring to who should be initially tended to in times of trouble. Rama's exile to the forest was an emergency situation in their marriage, so the Lord wanted to protect His wife first.

Sita Devi, on the other hand, wanted no such protection. She wanted to follow the Lord to the forest, for Rama was her very life and soul. She countered His arguments on propriety with her own. In pleading with her husband, she told Him that she would walk ahead of Him in the forest and protect Him. This isn't very surprising coming from Sita, since she was a great devotee of the Lord. Most of us initially approach God for some personal benefit.

"O best among the Bharatas [Arjuna], four kinds of pious men render devotional service unto Me—the distressed, the desirer of wealth, the inquisitive, and he who is searching for knowledge of the Absolute." (Lord Krishna, Bhagavad-gita, 7.16)

On a higher level, when one becomes a devotee, he or she no longer asks things from God, but instead offers things to Him. Sita was a delicate woman not used to the hardships of forest life, but she showed that she was as tough and renounced as the greatest of yogis. Having been married for so many years, her love for Rama hadn't dwindled a bit. It was she who was offering romantic gestures in the most difficult of times. Even later in life when she would be abandoned by Rama, she never stopped thinking of Him and loving Him. This illustrates the power of devotional service. Devotees of the God never stop loving Him and are always thinking of new ways to show their love. By always keeping their minds fixed on the lotus feet of the Lord, they are always with God and He is always with them. Being forever engaged in Krishna's service, one truly does live happily ever after.

The King of Kings

155

"The material defects of mistakes, illusions, cheating and sensory inefficiency do not exist in the words of the Supreme Personality of Godhead." (Lord Chaitanya, Chaitanya Charitamrita, Adi-lila 7.107)

Comment: *What kind of God is Lord Rama if He betrayed His wife Sita by sending her to live in Valmiki's ashrama?*

Response: Lord Rama, the incarnation of God in the Treta Yuga, did indeed renounce His wife towards the end of His time on earth. The couple had ruled over Ayodhya as king and queen for many many years prior to Sita Devi being sent to live in the hermitage of Maharishi Valmiki, Rama's great devotee and official biographer. Actions speak louder than words, and this act of the Rama's may seem to be wrong on the surface, but we should understand that the Lord is incapable of committing mistakes.

When examining the Lord's life and pastimes, we shouldn't cherry pick certain incidents, while ignoring others. Rama was on earth for a long time and performed many heroic deeds, so we should study all His pastimes before we have the nerve to pass judgment. Beginning from the time prior to His advent and continuing through His last days on earth, the Lord was completely dedicating to serving the needs of His devotees. In fact, Lord Vishnu decided to come to earth in human form only at the behest of the demigods who were terrified of the Rakshasa demon Ravana. God is great and completely self-satisfied, so He has no need to do anything, but in order to please His votaries, He comes to earth from time to time to give them protection and reinstitute the principles of dharma or religiosity. Born in the line of pious kings known as the Ikshvakus, Rama was intent on maintaining the prestigious family traditions. His father was the very well respected Maharaja Dashratha of Ayodhya. Dashratha was often addressed as the "Lord of Earth", for his fame and prowess was known throughout. In order to maintain the good name of His father, Lord Rama agreed to live in exile from the kingdom for a period of fourteen years. Dashratha had previously promised his youngest wife Kaikeyi any two boons of her choosing, so he couldn't renege when Kaikeyi asked for Rama to be banished. The Lord was the eldest son of the king, and next in line for the throne. He easily could have thrown a hissy-fit, refusing to accept His father's words, but He didn't. He voluntarily accepted a renounced order of life simply to honor the good name of His father and His ancestors.

Lord Rama's wife Sita, the most chaste and beautiful woman to ever have lived, insisted on accompanying the Lord for the duration of the exile period. Rama wanted very much to protect His wife from the dangers lurking in the woods, but she was up to the challenge, not wanting to live without her husband. Rama's younger brother Lakshmana also insisted on following Him, for he was ever attached to his elder brother. In this way, Rama allowed both of them to accompany Him simply to satisfy them and not Himself. Later on, after Sita was kidnapped by Ravana, the Lord enlisted the help of the Vanara king Sugriva. Sugriva had lost his kingdom due to a dispute with his brother Vali. Lord Rama helped Sugriva regain his throne by killing Vali while the two brothers were engaged in battle. For a kshatriya, one belonging to the warrior caste, such an action was against the proper code of conduct. An enemy shouldn't be attacked while engaged in battle with another. Yet Rama was more than willing to break this rule so that His dependent, Sugriva, could prosper. Once again, the Lord was acting in the interest of His devotees and not Himself.

After successfully defeating Ravana and reclaiming His wife, Lord Rama lived happily as the king of Ayodhya for thousands of years alongside Sita. However, one day one of the citizens had a gripe with Rama over the fact that He took Sita back after she had lived in the house of another, that being Ravana. According to the rules of propriety, such an act was prohibited. Upon hearing this, the Lord decided to send Sita to live with Valmiki Muni in the forest. This was in no way a slight on Sita, for she was a perfect devotee and wife. Ravana was never able to touch her, for she proved her purity through a fire ordeal. However, the Lord wanted to protect the good name of His father and His ancestors, so that is why He chose the course that He did. Rama wanted to set a good example for His fellow citizens. Unlike politicians of today who feel they are above the law, kings of the past wanted to be very pious. If they set a good example, then the rest of the citizens would follow and society would be peaceful.

The true fact of the matter is that devotees can never be separated from God. As long as one constantly has the Lord on their mind, thinking about Him, praying to Him, and singing His glories, then they are always with the Lord.

"...he who is situated in knowledge of Me I consider verily to dwell in Me. Being engaged in My transcendental service, he attains Me." (Lord Krishna, Bhagavad-gita, 7.18)

When Lord Krishna personally came to earth some five thousand years ago, He also had to leave His closest consort, Shrimati Radharani. Though He grew up in Vrindavana with all the other cowherd boys and girls, His duties later in life forced Him to go to Mathura and subsequently to Dvaraka, where He played the role of a king. Radharani was forced to live in separation from the Lord, but we should understand that the two are always together. God and His immediate expansions Radha, Sita, Lakshmi, etc. are always with Him and that is why they are referred to as eternal consorts. Even Lord Chaitanya renounced His wife at a very young age to take to the *sannyasa* order of life so that He could preach the original Hare Krishna movement throughout India. Though renounced by her husband, Vishnupriya had her mind always fixed on the lotus feet of Shri Krishna Chaitanya and in this way they were never truly separated.

Atheists and other *asuras* love to find fault with Lord Krishna, Rama, and other forms of God, for they themselves are reprobates by nature and view God as a threat to their sinful way of life. Though Krishna and His devotees don't bother them at all, these atheists still take any opportunity they can get to try to tear down the established principles and traditions of dharma as enjoined in the *shashtras*. These demons have always been around, for in the past they took the forms of Ravana, Shishupala, Kamsa, etc. It's up to the devotees of the Lord to stand up to these demons of today by cutting their words with our sharp logic and reason. We don't need any fancy weaponry, for our devotion and love for God is enough to defeat this enemy. Lakshmana dedicated his whole life to serving and protecting his brother, and we should follow in His footsteps. Lord Rama is our king forever and ever, and we will always love Him and His wife Sita.

Blanket For The Soul

"...He is as radiant as the autumn moon. His left side is embraced by mother Lakshmidevi, and His form is the shelter of all opulences, both material and spiritual." (*Sri Nrsimha-kavaca-stotram*)

The summer season is nice but pretty soon winter will return, bringing along its many pains and discomforts. One of the good things about winter is that it affords us the opportunity to really appreciate sleep, for we tend to sleep longer each night during the winter as opposed to the other seasons. Since we are so cold at night, our blankets provide us the comfort and warmth that we need to fall asleep fast.

It is such an enjoyable feeling to wrap ourselves in our blanket and fall asleep, knowing that we are fully protected from the cold. Since we tend to sleep longer in the winter, waking up is harder to do in the mornings because it means removing ourselves from the protection provided by our blanket. When we sleep, our mind is transferred from our gross material body to our subtle body, represented by the dreaming state. When we dream, we imagine that we really are in different surroundings and we completely forget that we actually are lying in our beds asleep.

"...this body will change. *Tatha dehantara-praptih*. And we have to change that body after death according to my mental condition because we have got two bodies, the subtle body and the gross body. This gross body is finished; it is no more working. Just like at night the gross body does not work. We are thinking, 'I am sleeping.' Sleeping means the body is so much tired, it is no more working. But your another body, which is made of mind, intelligence, and ego—subtle body—that is working. Everyone has got this experience. The subtle body takes you to another place or another condition." (Shrila Prabhupada, Lecture, 750615SB.HON)

Along with our nice mattress and pillows, our blankets are what allow us to comfortably enter into this sleeping state, for without it the effects of the bitter cold would be augmented. The warmth of the blanket is so nice that many of us try to artificially create a cold atmosphere even in the summer through the use of air conditioners and mechanical fans, in order that they may enjoy the benefits of our blanket.

Similar to the winter, this material world is constantly providing a chill to the living entities. According to the Vedas, we are not this body, but we are actually spirit souls, *aham brahmasmi*. Our natural constitutional position is that of bliss and knowledge, but due to our contact with material nature, we are forced to suffer the fourfold miseries of birth, death, old age, and disease. We are always trying to adjust our material condition so that we can try to feel some sort of happiness, making plan after plan, but our efforts eventually fail. No material plan can give us true peace of mind, thus we are left to suffer. The only way for us to get out of this misery is to elevate our consciousness to a platform where we are always thinking about God.

Just as the blanket provides us protection while we sleep, the Vedas provide us protection from the ignorance brought upon by *maya*, God's illusory energy that pervades the material world. The Vedas are the ancient scriptures of India originating from God Himself, passed down from time immemorial through the *parampara* system.

"The Blessed Lord said: I instructed this imperishable science of yoga to the sun-god, Vivasvan, and Vivasvan instructed it to Manu, the father of mankind, and Manu in turn instructed it to Ikshvaku." (Lord Krishna, Bhagavad-gita, 4.1)

Since they contain perfect knowledge, the Vedas are the best form of protection for the soul. In the Puranas, there are many different *kavachas* listed, each specific to a particular form of God or one of His associates. A *kavacha* is a shield given in the form of a mantra.

One who recites a specific *kavacha* with faith and reverence will enjoy the protection that it affords. One of the more famous *kavachas* is the "Sri Nrsimha-kavaca-stotram". Found in the Brahmanda Puranana, it is recited daily by many Vaishnavas.

"I shall now recite the Narasimha-kavacha, formerly spoken by Prahlada Maharaja. It is most pious, vanquishes all kinds of impediments, and provides one all protection."

Lord Narasimha Deva is the half-man half-lion incarnation of Krishna that specifically came to earth to give protection to His five year old devotee Prahlada, who was being harassed by his atheistic father Hiranyakashipu. Lord Narasimha Deva removes all fears from His devotees who sincerely seek out His protection.

In this age, the easiest way to receive God's protection is to constantly chant His holy names,

"Hare Krishna Hare Krishna, Krishna Krishna, Hare Hare, Hare Rama Hare Rama, Rama Rama, Hare Hare"

This method may seem simplistic, but it is very effective. There is no difference between God and His name. By chanting, we are directly connecting with God, and we are asking Him to allow us to love Him. In this way, we are transporting our souls from the material world to the spiritual world.

Appreciating the benefits of our blanket requires us to be in a position where we really need it. This position is naturally provided to us by Mother Nature in the form of winter. In a similar fashion, for us to truly appreciate chanting the names of God, we must be in a position of discomfort and frustration. Luckily for us, this situation is also naturally provided to us in this current age of Kali. According to the Vedas, the time period we are currently in is known as the age of quarrel and hypocrisy. Observing society, we can see that the Vedas are correct on this point. So chanting is very effective in this age, as stated by Lord Chaitanya, and it is the best way to connect with God. Doing so will give us the ultimate comfort...that of going back home, back to Godhead.

Transcending Sin

"Abandon all varieties of religion and just surrender unto Me. I shall deliver you from all sinful reaction. Do not fear." (Lord Krishna, Bhagavad-gita, 18.66)

Lord Jesus Christ is the founder of the modern day Christian religion. As the son of God, he was a dedicated preacher of God consciousness at a time when religion was on the decline. He challenged the established practices of society and begged people to put all their faith and trust in God. A preacher of the Vaishnava mold, he was so fearless in his efforts that he even willingly accepted crucifixion and forgave those who caused his death.

Christians commonly believe that Jesus died for their sins. This is definitely true, for a bona fide preacher spreading the message of God voluntarily accepts all the risks associated with such service. A preacher has no fear of even going to hell as long as God is satisfied with the work being done. However, just because Jesus died for our sins, does it mean that we should continue to willfully commit sins? America and much of the world has descended into a sinner's paradise. Innocent cows are slaughtered by the millions each year, babies are being aborted in the womb, gambling is becoming more and more acceptable, and intoxication is so common that there is even a growing movement to increase the number of legalized drugs. Smoking cigarettes and drinking alcohol are legal activities, though regulated, but apparently those forms of intoxication aren't enough. There is now a growing movement to legalize marijuana sale and use. Many are already smoking it illegally under the radar of the government.

So sinful life is very common today and leaders of the major religions don't seem to be doing much to curb it. In Christianity, the proposed solution is to have those identified as "sinners" attend confessional meeting with priests. "Forgiven me father, for I have sinned" is how these sessions are generally started. Now this is a very nice system, for we should all beg forgiveness for our sins. Thinking of God in that way, we can purify ourselves. However, we see that many people don't even bother attending confessionals, and if they do, they go right back to sinning after the session. Thus the system hasn't proved to be very effective. Simple forgiveness is not enough. We should mold our lives in such a way so as to stop such sinful activity.

If confessionals don't work, then what else can be done? How do we solve the problem? The Vedas tell us that there are four primary components to sinful life: meat eating, intoxication, gambling, and illicit sex. The regulative principles of devotional service state that one should refrain from these activities. Vedic literature also discusses various sins and means for atonement at great length. For example, if a brahmana, one who belongs to the priestly class of men, should happen to drink alcohol, it is recommended that he should force himself to drink burning hot alcohol as a means of punishment and atonement. There are many similar processes of atonement ranging from standing neck deep in cold water to fasting for days at a time, each of these relating to specific sins. These processes may represent a more potent form of sin eradication, but they still aren't one hundred percent effective.

Lord Krishna appeared on this earth as Lord Rama many thousands of years ago. Born as the eldest son of the great king of Ayodhya, Dashratha, Rama was the heir apparent to the throne. The king had decided to hand over the kingdom to Rama, but on the day set for the installation, Dashratha was forced to change his mind due to a promise he had made to his youngest wife, Kaikeyi. Instead of being the new king, Lord Rama was ordered to live in the forest as a recluse for fourteen years. After such time had passed, He would then be allowed to return to the kingdom. Upon being given this directive, the Lord went to His palace to gather His things and inform His wife, Sita Devi, of the news. Rama told Sita to remain in the kingdom and faithfully serve the elders and the new king-to-be, Rama's younger brother Bharata. Sita heard Rama's request, and she immediately rejected it. She begged the Lord to take her with Him to the forest. As part of her plea, Sita confidently asserted that she was completely sinless and that the Lord should never forsake such a person.

"Do you confidently take me with you, Oh great hero. Just as the water left after drinking, you should renounce your impatience and indignation. There exists no sin in me." (Sita Devi speaking to Lord Rama, Valmiki Ramayana, Ayodhya Kand, Sec 27)

Sita Devi was the incarnation of Goddess Lakshmi, the wife of Lord Narayana, or God. Raised in the kingdom of Maharaja Janaka, she was completely pure at heart and well versed in all the rules of propriety. However, it was not for this reason that she was sinless. Her greatest attribute was that she was completely devoted to Lord Rama, who was God Himself. From Sita's example, we can see how one can actually transcend sinful life. Sin can never touch one who is completely devoted to God and who lovingly serves Him. In the Bhagavad-gita, Lord Krishna's final instruction to Arjuna was that he should surrender unto Him, become His devotee, and thus become free from all sinful reactions.

Sita knew all the rituals and rites pertaining to the Vedas, and she strictly followed them. However, her devotion to her husband superseded all of that. Lord Rama gave her all these reasons why she should remain at home, but Sita rejected all of them since she was completely Krishna conscious. Lord Rama eventually relented and allowed Sita to accompany Him in exile. The Lord is actually with all of us through His expansion as the Supersoul or Paramatma. Keeping our minds always fixed upon Him and connecting with the Supersoul, we will realize that God is our constant companion.

"Just fix your mind upon Me, the Supreme Personality of Godhead, and engage all your intelligence in Me. Thus you will live in Me always, without a doubt." (Lord Krishna, Bhagavad-gita, 12.8)

From Sita Devi's example, we learn the one and only foolproof method of transcending sin. If we take to the process of devotional service by lovingly chanting the Lord's name, hearing stories about Him, and offering Him prayers, then we will become truly sinless and God will always be with us.

Enough is Enough

"After many births and deaths, he who is actually in knowledge surrenders unto Me, knowing Me to be the cause of all causes and all that is. Such a great soul is very rare." (Lord Krishna, Bhagavad-gita, 7.19)

Drug and alcohol addiction is a major problem in America and throughout the world. People become so dependent on their preferred form of intoxication that it consumes their lives. Addiction affects people from all walks of life, from the rich and the poor to the young and the old.

Curing these addictions is not an easy task. Bad habits form over a long period of time, making them very difficult to break. Depression, family pressures, and other personal problems lead people to become addicted to drinking alcohol or taking drugs. Drug rehabilitation centers have proved to be the most effective means for curing people's dependencies. These centers provide in depth counseling and treatment to those in need, all in a comfortable yet serious environment. Celebrities such as radio talk show host Rush Limbaugh and James Hetfield, lead singer of the heavy metal band Metallica, have attended these rehab centers and described how they changed their lives. The treatment providers really dig deep into the patient's psyche to find the real reason why they are addicted to drugs. The pressures of celebrity and fame are removed and the patients are in an environment where they can be truly open about their problems. For both Limbaugh and Hetfield, the diagnosed problem revolved around the pressures of celebrity and pleasing friends and family. They both felt immense pressure to live up to their celebrity image in their personal life. Unable to please family and friends, they grew resentful and took to intoxication as a means of curing their pain.

The key to curing any addiction is to stop denying the problem and to completely surrender. One must admit that he has a problem before any progress can be made. Friends and family can try to intervene, but even their best efforts will bear no fruit unless and until the person is willing to come to terms with their problem. Only then can they begin the healing process.

In a similar fashion, we are all entangled in this material world, repeatedly going through the cycle of birth and death based on our karma.

"As a person puts on new garments, giving up old ones, similarly, the soul accepts new material bodies, giving up the old and useless ones." (Lord Krishna, Bhagavad-gita, 2.22)

The Vedas tell us that this human form of life is unique in that it affords us the opportunity to understand God. Having a relationship with God and learning to love Him is our only permanent way out of this material world. There are 8,400,000 different varieties of species, each having their own level of intelligence. The animals are concerned primarily with eating, sleeping, mating, and defending. Where will my food come from? Where will I sleep? Who will I have sex with? After these three problems have been solved, then the animal must protect what it has. We human beings are supposed to be smarter than the animals, thus we shouldn't try to imitate them. Instead of worrying about which restaurant to eat at, what kind of mattress to buy next, or which girl to chase after, we should be concerned with why we are here and what happens to us after we die. Now granted, eating and sleeping are required for our sustenance, but they shouldn't be our primary concern. If we live a simple lifestyle then we will have more time to contemplate the real problems of life, they being birth, old age, disease and death.

Our main stumbling block is that most of us aren't aware that we have a problem. The material world has that effect on us. Lord Krishna, the Supreme Personality of Godhead, has created an illusory energy in this material world, which is known as *maya*. *Maya* makes us falsely think that we are all gods and that we are responsible for everything that we do and everything that happens to us. We are responsible to a small degree, because we have a minute amount of independence in controlling how our senses interact with nature. However, the results of our work are determined by karma and other people's karma. We are not the doer.

"Eat, drink and be merry" is how the saying goes. The Declaration of Independence of the United States contains the following words:

"We hold these truths to be self-evident, that all men are created equal, that they are endowed by their Creator with certain unalienable Rights, that among these are Life, Liberty and the pursuit of Happiness."

Now this is definitely true. God has surely granted us life, liberty, and the right to pursue happiness. The question that remains is how one should actually go about becoming happy. Material life means constantly hankering and lamenting. We keep making adjustments in the hopes that we will have peace of mind. Even if we are materially well off and living comfortably, that comfort will be gone at the time of death. According to the Vedic teachings, we will be forced to take another body after death, but our previously accumulated wealth doesn't come with us.

True spiritual understanding only comes when we realize the existence of this repetitious cycle. We know for a fact that our ancestors have died and some of our relatives have even died during our lifetime. Witnessing this, we still try to pretend that we will live forever. Death is guaranteed, so we should be inquisitive to find out what happens to the soul after it leaves this body. Luckily for us, Lord Krishna, God Himself, has explained all of this in the Bhagavad-gita. If we take the time to read this wonderful book and make a sincere effort in trying to understand it, then we will surely be cured of our material disease and thus achieve everlasting happiness.

Krishnaloka

"Krishna is the cause of all causes. He is the primal cause, and He is the very form of eternal being, knowledge and bliss." (Brahma-samhita)

Whether we are in school or working hard at our jobs, we all look forward to vacations. Vacations provide us relief from the daily grind, a way to break free from the monotony of everyday life. We just can't wait to have some time off, where we aren't pressured to meet deadlines or required to be at a certain place at a specific time.

When we were growing up as children attending school, the Christmas and summer breaks were the two longest vacation periods in American schools anyway. Going to school is something most kids don't like to do, so getting to stay home, wake up later, and watch television all day brings great joy to students. Even His Divine Grace A.C. Bhaktivedanta Swami Prabhupada, the founder of the modern day Hare Krishna movement, had a dislike for school when he was a child.

"I never wanted to go to school. And my father was very kind. 'So all right. Why you are not going to school?' I would say, 'I will go tomorrow.' 'All right.' But my mother was very careful. Perhaps if my mother would not have been little strict, I would not have gotten any education. My father was very lenient. So she used to force me. One man would take me to school. Actually, children do not want to go to school. They want to play. Against the will of the children, he has to go to school. Then there is examination, not only going to school." (Shrila Prabhupada, Lecture, 740621.BG.GER)

Adults working full-time have fewer vacation periods, so they usually try to make better use of their time off than children do. Getaways to exotic destinations, site seeing, or visiting theme parks are some of the more popular vacation ideas. Disneyworld is the probably the world's most famous vacation resort getaway.

"Walt Disney World Resort is the most visited and largest recreational resort in the world, containing four theme parks; two water parks; twenty-three themed hotels; and numerous shopping, dining, entertainment and recreation venues. Owned and operated by the Walt Disney Parks and Resorts segment of The Walt Disney Company, it is located southwest of Orlando, Florida. The property is often abbreviated Walt Disney World, Disney World or WDW, and is often referred to by locals as simply Disney." (Wikipedia)

Kids especially love going there so they can see all their favor Disney characters along with riding roller coasters such as the one on Space Mountain. Adults even enjoy Disneyworld for all the sites and attractions that it offers. Planning such trips gives us something to look forward to. The opportunity to explore new places and break free from the daily routine gives us excitement. Looking forward to things is an essential part of maintaining a healthy mindset. Staying at fancy hotels, fine dining, and relaxing on a beach are very nice activities, but wouldn't it be better to always be on vacation? Instead of looking for ways to break out of our daily routines, wouldn't it be more beneficial to change our daily routine to include fun activities? This may seem impossible to us, but according to the Vedic teachings, this is exactly what results from practicing devotional service.

We may not be aware of it, but we are all serving something or someone, for this is what we are born to do. We serve our family, friends, countrymen, and even our own senses. It is the natural position of the spirit soul to serve, and it is the natural position of God to be served. By practicing bhakti yoga, or devotional service, we gradually elevate ourselves to where we are in complete God consciousness. When we are always thinking about God and lovingly serving Him, then in our minds, we are always on vacation. Serving our senses may provide us temporary happiness, but service to God brings about everlasting bliss. Lord Krishna is described as having an eternally blissful body, *saccidananda vigraha*. He is always in bliss because His knowledge is perfect. If we dedicate our time to serving Him, then we can come in contact with that knowledge. If God is eternally blissful, then naturally anyone who comes into contact with Him will also be full of bliss and happiness.

Chanting God's names, reading books about Him, and offering Him food are extremely fun activities. God is very nice and He takes care of us when we come to Him. Krishna's abode is completely spiritual, and when we serve Him, we become guests in His spiritual home. He is the most hospitable host, so if we visit Him once, we will never want to leave.

Sometimes when we are on vacation, we overindulge ourselves in eating, drinking, and sleeping. Some people often joke that they need a vacation from their vacation. Unlike material activities, one never gets tired of devotional service. The expansive Vedic literature provides us the opportunity to always read stories about Lord Krishna, the Supreme Personality of Godhead. These stories are timeless and through them, we always associate with God. So let us commence the process of devotional service and we'll be guaranteed a spot in the greatest vacation resort, the spiritual planet of Krishnaloka.

Rama's Protection

"Whether it be residence on top of a place, traveling on airplanes, or flying through the sky (via yogic powers), in all circumstances the shade of the husband's feet is by far superior." (27.9)

prāsāda agraiḥ vimānaiḥ vā vaihāyasa gatena vā |

sarva avasthā gatā bhartuḥ pādac cāyā viśiṣyate

It is part of a wife's nature to be subservient to her husband and to willingly put herself under his protection. Women naturally prefer to be taken care of and provided for by their loving husbands. On the reverse side, men naturally like to protect and care for women. Women instinctively known this and that's why it is often seen that a woman will sometimes knowingly pretend to be ignorant on certain topics, in the hopes that they can cajole a man into helping them. The man is more than happy to show the woman the proper way, and garnering such attention, a woman feels more attracted to the man.

"Not *should be*. They *are*. You have become voluntarily subservient to your man. That is nature. They are seeking to become subservient by attracting a man: 'Take me as subservient.' That is natural." (Shrila Prabhupada answering question from a reporter on why women should be subservient to men)

This is the natural course of things, but the rise of the women's independence movement has brought a central paradigm shift. Over the past fifty years or so, women have been taught to be more independent and reject the help of men. They want to be seen as equals in all areas of society and want no such preferential treatment. This idea certainly is ideal since at our core, we are all equal. Though we falsely identify ourselves as men, women, black, white, American, or Indian, we are all spirit souls at our core, *aham brahmasmi*. Though spiritually we are all equal, due our different karmas, we have been put into different types of bodies. The material world is governed by three *gunas* or qualities: goodness, passion, and ignorance. Each one us possess these qualities to varying degrees, and thus we see the variations in body types and species. Men and women are equal spiritually, but the Vedas have given them separate and distinct roles to perform in order to attain spiritual perfection. Men are to be the protectors and women are to serve their husbands, a system which allows for peace and prosperity. Living happily this way, husband and wife can focus their time on becoming Krishna conscious, which is the ultimate aim of life.

Instead of making women happier, the independence movement has resulted in women being exploited.

"What have 'equal rights' and 'high profiles' brought women anyway? Exploitation, broken families, broken marriages, an animalistic chain of uncaring sexual partners, abortion, children bereft of parental love, and above all, no time for Krishna consciousness." (Visnupriya Devi Dasi, Back to Godhead Magazine #25-02, 1991)

Instead of being obliged to provide protection, a man can now satisfy his sexual urges by seducing a woman, and then leaving her aside afterwards. Women are left begging the men for more stable relationships, but the men have lost their desire to protect. Many times pregnant women aren't even protected and they are left asking for support from the government. Through the practice of casual sex, women who accidentally get pregnant are advised to kill the child in the womb, or to raise the child by themselves. Such activity definitely isn't good for society, and moreover it goes against human nature.

God came to earth in the form of a handsome and pious prince by the name of Rama many thousands of years ago in Ayodhya, India. Born in the royal family of the Ikshvakus, the Lord was the next in line to ascend the throne occupied at the time by His father Maharaja Dashratha. Due to unforeseen circumstances, Lord Rama was passed over for the throne and instead ordered to spend fourteen years in the forest as an exile from the kingdom. Being married to His wife Sita Devi at the time, the Lord advised her to remain in the kingdom for the duration of the fourteen years, for she would be better protected at home. The environments of a royal palace and that of the wilderness really have no similarities. The Lord was a valiant warrior, trained in the military arts by the great sage Vishvamitra. Also, since He was God Himself, living in the forest would be no problem for Him. He wanted very much for His wife to be protected, so He tried His best to dissuade her from following Him. Sita Devi however refused to abandon her husband in His time of need. She informed Him that she preferred the shade of the Lord's feet in all circumstances. By this, she meant that she always wanted her husband's protection, wherever it may be. For if the husband is there to protect the wife, then both parties are happy, and the wife feels completely at ease in any situation. The idea of independence didn't appeal to Sita at all.

Lord Rama is Krishna Himself, the Supreme Personality of Godhead. From this verse we understand that the shade of the Lord's feet is the greatest form of protection one can have. Sita Devi knew this and that's why she refused to live without the Lord. Sita Devi was one of the greatest devotees of the Lord. An incarnation of Goddess Lakshmi, her only dharma was to make Rama happy. It is ironic since the meaning of the name Rama is "one who gives pleasure", yet Sita wasn't just a taker of pleasure, she was a giver. God is capable of providing us the greatest pleasure, but the devotees' first inclination is to please the Lord. Just as the wife prefers the shade of her husband's feet, the devotee prefers the shade provided by chanting the Lord's holy name. In this age, if we always think of the Lord, hear stories about Him, and keep His name on the tip of our tongue, then the scorching hot rays of Kali Yuga can never burn us.

Music To Our Ears

"When there is sound vibrated praising the transcendental pastimes of the Lord...one is forced to hear. That hearing process enters into the mind, and the practice of yoga is automatically performed." (Shrila Prabhupada, Shrimad Bhagavatam, 3.28.19 Purport)

We live in an age where technology is rapidly improving, with new products coming out all the time. Big screen televisions, cellular telephones, Bluetooth devices, and laptop computers are some of the products that have resulted. One of the more intriguing advancements brought on by this advancement in technology is the mp3 music file.

No less than thirty years ago, music was listened to primarily on record players. Artists released albums on large vinyl disks and consumers would then play them on large turntable style record players. Unlike the compact portable music players that exist today, these record players were quite bulky. There were no fast forward or rewind buttons; instead you would have to manually move the needle or the stylus to a different position on the record. Listening to music in the car was accomplished only by turning on the radio. There was no freedom in that, for one was forced to listen to whatever music was playing on the various radio stations. Progress occurred gradually through the years with the release of cassette tapes, which was then followed by compact discs. This smaller medium made it easier to listen to music while on the go. Compact discs even afforded us the luxury to fast forward and rewind between tracks on albums.

Fast forward to today and we now have the luxury of listening to music stored on computer files, called mp3s. Though a compressed form of music, these files are almost identical in sound quality to compact discs and they provide us much more flexibility and convenience. A large library of music is now available to us right at our fingertips wherever we go. Mp3 files can also be tagged with metadata, such as artist, track, and album names. You can even apply an album cover image to mp3 files, allowing you to browse through covers on your iPod or computer, similar to the way people used to browse through record album covers in music stores. Listening to music has never been easier, and we can even copy and share these files with our friends.

According to the Vedic teachings, technological advancement is not completely shunned, but it is generally not viewed favorably. The reason for this is that new technology binds us in the mode of passion. The material world is governed by three *gunas* or qualities: goodness, passion, and ignorance. Lord Krishna describes the mode of passion in this way:

"O chief of the Bharatas, when there is an increase in the mode of passion, the symptoms of great attachment, uncontrollable desire, hankering, and intense endeavor develop." (Bhagavad-gita, 14.12)

One in the mode of passion is constantly hankering after things and is thus never satisfied. If one only focuses the mind on matters of sense gratification, then it will be very difficult to achieve spiritual advancement.

"In the mode of passion, people become greedy, and their hankering for sense enjoyment has no limit. One can see that even if one has enough money and adequate arrangement for sense gratification, there is neither happiness nor peace of mind." (Shrila Prabhupada, Bhagavad-gita, 14.17 Purport)

When we get a new phone or mp3 player, immediately we are anxiously awaiting the next release, hoping that newer technology will correlate to greater happiness. With our new device, we are happy for a few days while we discover all the new features. That satisfaction doesn't last for long however, as we eagerly await the release of the next model. Evidence of this can be seen with the iPhone produced by Apple.

Considered a groundbreaking device, the iPhone is a cellular telephone, mp3 player, navigation system, and internet web browser all rolled into one device. Its popularity is immense, and its utility far reaching. However, upon its initial release, people still complained about features that it lacked, such as cut-and-paste, and MMS messaging capabilities. In answer to that, Apple recently released a newer iPhone model, which was once again met with great approval. We can be sure the euphoria will be short-lived, for people will be eagerly anticipating the next groundbreaking device. Since our material senses can never be satisfied, we end up trapped in a never ending cycle of hankering and lamenting.

Though technology can have this binding effect, if we use it for serving Lord Krishna, the Supreme Personality of Godhead, then it becomes most beneficial to us. When we dovetail material activities with devotional service to God, then our material activities become spiritualized. Mp3 technology allows us to listen to songs about Krishna much more easily now. Since we are working hard at school or at our jobs, it may be difficult to find time to chant. Mp3 players allow us to listen to Hari-Kirtana, congregational songs about Krishna, at any place and at any time. We love to listen to music while driving, so now we have the opportunity to listen to songs praising Krishna. We can even sing along if we want. Car stereos now even support mp3 CDs, which allow one to place hundreds of tracks onto one disc. The car stereo will read and display the song title, name, and album, and it even keeps track of where you left off in a track when you start your car again. Such great technology shouldn't go to waste.

One can probably make the best use of mp3 technology by using it to listen to Krishnakatha, or discourses about Krishna. The recorded lectures of His Divine Grace A.C. Bhaktivedanta Swami Prabhupada give us direct access to such discourses. Shrila Prabhupada was a great devotee of Lord Krishna and the founder of the modern day Hare

Krishna movement. While starting the movement in the late 60s, he gave lectures daily on Krishna consciousness, and these were recorded by his disciples. All his recorded lectures, speeches, and spiritual conversations are now available on mp3 format. We should take advantage of this wonderful opportunity to have a real spiritual master give us instruction. The Vedas tell us that the hearing process is the most effective in receiving transcendental knowledge.

With the Prabhupada Mp3 Library, we can now take spiritual instruction wherever we may be. Prabhupada made the complex philosophy of Vedanta understandable to the common man. Just by hearing one lecture, our lives are greatly benefited. Listening a few minutes a day while driving, while at work, or while relaxing at home will make our lives so much better.

Ties That Bind

"One who can control his senses by practicing the regulated principles of freedom can obtain the complete mercy of the Lord and thus become free from all attachment and aversion." (Lord Krishna, Bhagavad-gita, 2.64)

Marriage really changes people, sometimes for the worst, but mostly for the better. The idea of independence and freedom vanishes, for one has to constantly meet the needs of their spouse. One's whole way of life changes, and though many marriages end in divorce, the institution itself has a positive impact on one's character.

For men, marriage is often dreaded. The modern concept of having a bachelor party prior to a wedding is a way for the groom-to-be to have one more night of fun prior to tying the knot. Many husbands often jokingly refer to their wife as the "ball and chain". Women generally have a different view of marriage. To them, it provides an added sense of security to their lives. Marriage allows women to have a stronger attachment to their men. Every girl dreams of the perfect wedding when they are little. They spend time thinking of the perfect arrangements, where to have the wedding, and what kind of dress they will wear. It is a very exciting event for them.

Either way, a successful marriage requires great effort from both parties. Sometimes the wife isn't happy with things that the husbands says or forgets to say. Other times, the husband isn't happy due to what he perceives as nagging and pestering from the wife. These are all issues that people learn to deal with through practice. Instead of doing whatever we want, we now must take into account the feelings of our spouse. The spouse is someone who lives with us, meaning we see them all the time. That makes it all the more important to make sure we have a friendly relationship with them, taking great care not to cause any enmity. Normally if we have a disagreement with one of our friends or colleagues, we can take a timeout period from them and then resume the friendship later on. We are not afforded that luxury in a marriage. Marriage means having to serve someone besides ourselves. Later on when children come into the picture, the responsibilities increase even more. Children require constant attention, leaving us no time for selfishness. In the long run, this is good for us. It teaches us to be detached from our own personal desires. This service makes us act even nicer to our other friends and family.

Similar to the demands of a marriage, the process of devotional service requires one to always attend to the needs of God. God actually doesn't have any needs, but through His mercy, He allows us to voluntarily take up His service for our benefit. Lord Krishna, the Supreme Personality of Godhead, is the reservoir of all pleasure. In this material world we are dedicated to serving our senses or the senses of others. This may give us temporary so called "happiness", but real happiness comes from service to Krishna. This is our original constitutional position, so it is not unnatural at all. When we are dedicated to offering food to Krishna, hearing stories about Him, or talking about Him with others, we forget our own desires. As a result, we feel the highest form of bliss.

Detachment brings about peace and happiness. If we are overly attached to material objects, we lose our composure and steadiness of mind. We see in professional sports that the most successful athletes are the ones that can stay focused even in the most pressure packed situations. People often joke that tennis great Roger Federer plays like a yogi, for he rarely loses his temper on court. While others throw rackets or verbally abuse umpires, Federer remains focused on the task at hand. For these athletes, the key to success lies in their detachment from the result of their activity. Winning and losing is important, but they don't feel overly dejected from losing nor do they overly rejoice over victories. Not everyone can become a high class athlete or great mystic, but we can still practice detachment. The easiest way to break free from material attachments is to take up the process of devotional service.

"...it is undoubtedly very difficult to curb the restless mind, but it is possible by constant practice and by detachment." (Lord Krishna, Bhagavad-gita, 6.35)

In a marriage, when we serve our spouse, we are always checking to see if they are happy or whether they still love us. If we start to doubt their love, we get angry and disagreements arise. When we serve Krishna, His love for us is guaranteed and never needs to be doubted. We have trouble maintaining one wife or one husband, but Krishna can maintain millions of devotees at the same time. Knowing this, we can go on serving Him and always be assured that He'll love us even more than we love Him. If we vow to always serve Lord Krishna with all our thoughts, words, and deeds, then we will become first class people.

Home Schooling

191

"I have been taught by my father and mother to follow my husband in all conditions of life, and I shall carry out now what I have been taught. I shall not abide by any other counsel." (Sita Devi speaking to Lord Rama, Valmiki Ramayana, Ayodhya Kand, Sec 27)

According to Vedic philosophy, women and shudras are considered the less intelligent class of people. They are given such a designation due to the fact that they traditionally didn't receive a formal education. Shudras are the working class of people in the *varnashrama* dharma system, which is the division of society and life stages based on a person's natural qualities. The four *varnas* are the brahmanas (priests), kshatriyas (warriors/administrators), vaishyas (merchants/farmers), and shudras (laborers). The four *ashramas* represent the progressive stages one goes through in life, namely the brahmacharya (celibate student life), grihastha (married life), vanaprastha (retired family life), and sannyasa (complete renunciation from family life).

In the ancient Vedic system, male children would be invested with the sacred thread which signaled the beginning of their second birth. Everyone's first birth is from their biological mother and father, but the second birth is more important since that is when spiritual education begins. Upon receiving the sacred thread, boys would then live with their spiritual master in what was known as the gurukula. The gurukula was *the* school system, with boys living there at no charge. Everyone needs food to survive, so in order to meet this demand, the students, known as brahmacharis, would go begging for food door to door from the grihastha or householder community. The collected food would then be given to the guru, who would in turn distribute it amongst his family and his students. In this way, people living in family life would support the schools and their students. At the gurukula, students would be taught on all subjects of life, but mainly on spiritual matters. They would be taught how to worship Lord Krishna, the Supreme

Personality of Godhead, and they would be imbibed with the highest understanding of the soul and its position relative to this material world.

Shudras and women would not attend gurukulas. Shudras are the laborer class of people so they don't require an education. Their duty is to serve the three higher *varnas*. The brahmanas, kshatriyas, and vaishyas in turn must do their part to provide complete protection to the shudras. Women would be provided protection in their youth by their father, and would then be married off as soon they reached the age when puberty starts. At that point, they would be protected by their husbands. It is for these reasons that women and shudras are frequently referred to as unintelligent in the Vedic literatures.

Lord Rama was an incarnation of Krishna, and thus was no different than God Himself. He advented on this earth many thousands of years ago in the town of Ayodhya and as part of His pastimes, He willingly accepted a punishment of exile into the forest from His father, Maharaja Dashrata, the king of Ayodhya. The Lord was married at the time to His beautiful and chaste wife Sita Devi. Rama informed her of the punishment and begged her to remain in the town for the duration of the exile period. He put forth all the pertinent arguments relating to the rules of propriety and also warned her of all the dangers of forest life. Sita Devi in turn completely rejected His arguments and put forth her own. She explained the proper duties of a wife and how she was taught to always serve her husband.

Now growing up as an "uneducated" woman, how did Sita have such a high understanding of these rules? Well, she explained to the Lord that these lessons were taught by her mother and father. Sita Devi was an incarnation of the goddess of fortune, Lakshmi. Lakshmi is always serving the Supreme Lord in the spiritual sky, and so when God comes to this earth, she naturally follows Him. Sita didn't have an ordinary birth, but was instead born from Mother Earth, who is known as Bhumi Devi. The highly exalted King Janaka found her when she was just a baby while he was plowing a field. He raised the girl as his own daughter and he treated her as his most precious jewel. Janaka had a world famous reputation for having the highest character and having his senses under control. Having such wonderful parents in Janaka and his wife Sunayana, Sita Devi received a world-class education at home, without needing to attend school.

In the modern world, gurukulas are almost nonexistent and most education takes place in public schools and universities. While these places may provide a nice education on material subjects, they don't teach anything about the soul or devotion to Krishna. So in actuality, people attending such institutions aren't receiving any worthwhile education. We are all growing up as shudras, not having taken our second birth. We learn from Sita Devi's example just how important it is to teach Krishna consciousness at home. Parents can start teaching their children about God at any age. It has been evidenced that children naturally take to the singing of the Lord's name, without any cajoling. A child can see a picture of Krishna and immediately understand that it is no ordinary picture, but that it is the Supreme Lord Himself. This is all due to past karma and life experiences. We are all originally devotees of Krishna, but somehow or other we have forgotten Him and are left to struggle in this material world. If parents allow their children to hear about Krishna, to chant His holy name, to eat His prasadam, and to offer prayers to Him, then they will grow up to be more intelligent than the greatest of PhD scholars.

God is the Most Magnanimous

"O Lakshmana, do you rule this earth with Me. You are like My second self, so this glorious opportunity has been presented to you as well. O Saumitra, do you enjoy all the pleasures you desire and the fruits of the regal life. My life and this kingdom I covet for your sake alone." (Lord Rama speaking to Lakshmana, Valmiki Ramayana, Ayodhya Kanda, 4.43-44)

Every now and then God personally comes to earth to deliver His devotees, giving them protection from the *asuras*. According to Vedic teachings, since the beginning of creation, there has been an ongoing war between the *daivas* and *asuras*. The *daivas* are those who believe in God and the *asuras* are God's enemies, the atheists. The atheists are very attached to sense gratification, taking this gross material body to be the be-all end-all. They view the *daivas* as a threat to their sinful way of life, thus they are always harassing them. The attacks of the *asuras* take various forms, sometimes they declare that God is dead, other times they say that He is impersonal and that we are all God, so we have no need to worship a Supreme Being. When they really feel threatened, the *asuras* revert to using force against the devotees.

This was the case many thousands of years ago, when a demon named Ravana had risen to power. A Rakshasa by birth, Ravana performed the severest of penances to gain the favor of the demigods. The *devatas*, or demigods, are God's deputies in charge of running the material world. One of their prime duties is to grant material benedictions to those who please them. These boons are granted to *anyone* who properly worships them. Lord Shiva known as Mahadeva, or the great demigod, has a reputation for being easily pleased. Regardless of the person's character, Lord Shiva will grant boons to those who pray to him and perform austerities. Ravana pleased not only Lord Shiva, but many other demigods. He received various boons, such as having ten heads, and being invincible in battle against any demigod. In his haste for acquisition of power, Ravana neglected to ask for immunity from human beings, thinking there was none who existed that could defeat him. Taking advantage of this oversight, the demigods went to Lord Vishnu, the Supreme Lord Himself, and asked Him to relieve their distress by ridding the world of Ravana.

The Lord kindly obliged and took birth as a human being by the name of Rama, the eldest son of the king of Ayodhya, Maharaja Dashratha. Ravana was not only very powerful, but he used his strength to harass the great sages living in the forests. During that time, the saintly people, the rishis, mostly lived in the forest, for that environment was better suited for their spiritual activities. Ravana and his band of Rakshasa demons went after these saints, killing them and then feasting upon their flesh. The atheists are always merciless, having no compassion even on the kindest of people. Lord Rama was born in a very famous family, known as the Ikshvakus. Not only were they all great kings, but they were terrific fighters, the highest of the kshatriya race. God specifically chose to take birth in this dynasty due its reputation and high standing.

When He reached an appropriate age, Lord Rama was set to be installed on the throne as the new king of Ayodhya by His father. Rama was eldest son and the most beloved of all the people, so the king desired very much to pass down the kingdom to Him. The news was spread throughout the city and everyone become very excited. When Rama was told of the news, He went to His younger brother Lakshmana and spoke the above mentioned verse. When God comes to earth, His closest associates come with Him. In Shvetadvipa, a planet in the spiritual world, Lord Narayana takes rest on Ananta Shesha, the serpent who holds all the planets of the universe on his unlimited hoods. Narayana is served by Goddess Lakshmi, His eternal consort. When the Lord took birth as Rama, Shesha and Lakshmi also took birth in the forms of Lakshmana and Sita respectively. From their childhood, Lakshmana was inseparable from Rama, for he would always follow his elder brother like a shadow.

When we devote ourselves completely to God, He recognizes our love and reciprocates. Being installed as the new king was the highest of honors bestowed on Lord Rama, but He made sure to include His younger brother. He never wanted Lakshamana to feel slighted in any way. Obviously Lakshmana was also very happy on this occasion and needed no consolation, but the Lord, out of His generous nature, told Lakshmana that the two would rule the earth together. Sometimes when one ascends the ladder of fame and fortune, the "little" people are sometimes forgotten. The new fame and celebrity can cause relationships with friends and family to change. But God always loves His devotees, no matter what. Lord Rama wanted to assure His younger brother that he would also enjoy all the luxuries associated with being king.

Even though God separates Himself from His devotees from time to time, they are never without Him. Lord Krishna had to leave the gopis of Vrindavana and later on He had to leave His friends Arjuna and Uddhava. Lord Rama was forced to abandon His wife Sita, who had done no wrong. Sometimes His duties require Him to follow a certain path, but He never forgets His devotees. They are always thinking of Him and He is always with them in spirit.

"The yogi who knows that I and the Supersoul within all creatures are one, worships Me and remains always in Me in all circumstances." (Lord Krishna, Bhagavad-gita, 6.31)

God is always looking to glorify His devotees first, thus this behavior on the part of Rama towards Lakshmana wasn't very surprising. Lord Krishna delivered the message of the Bhagavad-gita to Arjuna, so as to give him everlasting fame as a great devotee. Hanuman was deputed to find the whereabouts of Sita and to destroy Lanka at the behest of Lord Rama. For this reason, he is loved and adored to this very day. Bhishmadeva's devotion to Krishna was rewarded at the time of his death, when Krishna granted him the opportunity to give spiritual instruction to Yudhishthira, the eldest of the Pandava brothers.

"Krishna wanted the Pandavas to hear from Bhishma, who alone was able to give such great instructions even at the time of his death. So, Krishna likes to glorify His devotee." (Shrila Prabhupada)

Though we may suffer through hard times or witness the calamities of others, we should never forget that God is nice. Any service rendered to Him never goes to waste.